THE DEAD BEDROOM FIX

(THIRD EDITION)

By Ralph B.
(aka "D.S.O.")

helpformen.com

WHO THIS BOOK IS FOR

This book was written for heterosexual men who are in long-term monogamous relationships and want more sex. Yes, I realize that there is a growing phenomenon of women being frustrated with their own lackluster sex lives. Sorry, ladies. This book is not for you.

If you are a woman and your libido is outpacing that of your husband/boyfriend, I can save you a lot of time and money and give you some quick solutions to try out:

Concentrate on making yourself look young (as young as possible) and pretty. Yes, it's shallow and stupid. We're talking about MEN here. There is a reason why I listed this first. Don't overthink things. Men are visual creatures. Just look at porn, strip clubs, your husband's eyes as that young pretty gal walks by him, etc. Yes, the shallow stuff matters. A lot. I know you think less of him because of this little fact… but that's human nature. There's a lot about female human nature that men don't appreciate, but we're trying to do our best here to get along and make this relationship work, right? Sometimes we need to set our feelings aside and be more pragmatic about these things. "My husband likes pretty women… maybe I should work on being prettier."

Don't be a controlling asshole. Nothing is more of a turnoff than a nagging, emasculating woman. Try empathy and sweetness instead. Be bouncy, playful, and fun. Be his oasis in a world that seems to try its best to bring him down. Give up control and let him take over every now and then. Yes, he will make mistakes. He's human, after all. Nobody is perfect. Don't freak out on him and shame him for trying to help and trying to be a better man. Never, ever punish good behavior. The net positive return from you giving up control is far greater than the negative impact of a few silly mistakes on his part.

Loosen up. Go with the flow. Enjoy life. Enjoy your husband. Be a cool, sexy chick. Submissiveness and joy are attractive.

Encourage him. I know he annoys the shit out of you half the time and you've lost a great deal of respect for him over the years, but he's your man and you want more sex, right?

Is he watching and masturbating to porn regularly? Unfortunately, excessive porn consumption can be addictive. It can drain him of his energy and have profoundly negative effects on his well-being and behavior. Want to be different and sexy? Watch porn with him. Yes, seriously. Make it one of many dirty, secret things you two do together as a couple. Tell him what you like. Tell him YOU want to be his porn star.

None of the above issues apply to your situation? Tell him to get his testosterone checked. It's not natural for a dude to turn down sex repeatedly. He should want it frequently. Something is up and it MIGHT be that his hormones are out of balance and he needs a simple tune-up. Many women report that they "got their husband back" after he started a regimen of testosterone replacement therapy. While he's at it, have him check all his other blood markers, as well: thyroid, blood lipids, etc.

There's your dead bedroom fix, ladies. If these don't work, it's time to move on. You're a woman. Let's be honest here… you could get sex this afternoon if you wanted to. It's a totally different ballgame for men. We have a MUCH harder time trying to convince the ladies in our lives to allow us access to their bodies. You literally just have to open the door and yell, "Who wants some of this?!" Some dummy will come running to your door.

Now, kindly go away. We men need to chat about you behind your back. You are WAY more complicated than we are and this will take an entire book to break down.

BEFORE WE GET STARTED

… let's get some important things out of the way.

1. I'm going to assume your wife is healthy. It may seem obvious to most of you, but I have heard more than a few times:

- *"Well, it all started when my wife was diagnosed with breast cancer…"*

- *"She suffers from depression and was recently put on meds. Since then, she has no libido."*

- *"We had a baby one month ago. It was a very rough pregnancy. Cesarian. We almost lost the baby. Now she has zero interest in sex."*

Give the woman a break! The poor thing is a human being. Those are big roadblocks in the way of her sexual desire. Give her time and have some empathy. Be a partner to her. Get her the help that she needs.

In sickness and in health, remember?

2. I'm going to assume that YOU are healthy. If you have issues that impact your day-to-day life (chronic disease, hormonal issues, mental health issues, etc.), then your situation is officially above my pay grade. Get those issues ironed out and then come back to this book. You have bigger fish to fry, my friend.

3. You need to set aside your preconceptions of what both increases and erodes the sexual desire within your wife. You need to set aside your notions of what she SHOULD do as your wife and partner. You need to set aside these crippling thoughts about what you DESERVE as her man. What you've done so far is flat out not working, so it's time for Plan B. You need a whole new mindset.

Stop reading online stories from men talking about their all-too-common "low libido" and "asexual" wives and "that's just how marriage is." Ninety percent of the time those stories are from men who just don't get it. They will never get it. Don't become part of the long line of men trying like hell to join the growing "I AM A HELPLESS VICTIM" parade. Stay away from these people. Their mindset is poisonous. They WILL infect you! (See the Dead Bedrooms group on Reddit, for example.)

4. You may be offended by what you read in this book. Some of the things I say may seem a bit "out there." They may even seem offensive. Sexist. Bone-headed. Antiquated. Misogynistic.

Fine, I get it. Really, I do. I was in your shoes years ago and would've laughed at a book like this back then. I was way too "smart" and "educated." I knew better. Hindsight is 20/20, of course.

All I can tell you is that this WORKS. Feelings be damned… you need solutions. From my experience, what I outline in this book is the best and most direct path to getting the sex you feel you need.

INTRODUCTION
MY STORY

I'm a forty-something divorced (and now remarried) dad of four kids. I have three from my first marriage and one from my second. As of this writing, their ages range from three to twenty-one years of age.

Yes, I'm a busy man.

I work more than full-time, thanks to the busy nature of Help for Men and Dad Starting Over. I also cook, clean, fold clothes, help with homework, play, discipline, chauffeur, counsel, etc. The job of husband and father never ends.

Being a divorced and remarried father of four is not exactly the life I planned for myself. It is, at times, really freaking exhausting. To say my adult life has been filled with dramatic ups and downs would be an understatement.

Before becoming divorced-and-remarried dad extraordinaire, I endured a fifteen-year marriage that could be described as "roommates who once in a blue moon had sex that resulted in babies." My ex-wife was, apparently, one very fertile woman and I was one very fertile dude. Don't let my three kids from my first marriage convince you that our sex life was abundant. It wasn't. At all. It was, by definition, a very "dead bedroom."

My ex-wife would often say: *"I don't know why I don't feel like having sex. I just don't."*

To make a very long and very painful story short, fifteen years into our marriage (and after twenty years as a couple) she was caught in a physical affair with another man. I regrettably found out ALL of the dirty little details. (Thank you, smartphone technology.) Yes, I caught the affair early on, but my "low libido" wife was still more than able to muster up enough energy to get a WHOLE LOT of crazy sex done in those few short months.

After I saw the evidence of the affair and all of the dirty details, I said what every man in my position says:

"She did THAT with HIM? She would never do THAT with ME?!"

I endured years of almost zero intimacy during our marriage. I thought the kind of closeness, affection, and filthy sex I craved only happened in dirty movies. I was very wrong. The real-life porn movie was happening alright… but my character didn't have a role in those sexy scenes. My scenes involved changing diapers and mowing the lawn. I felt cheated. I felt like a dumb schmuck that was taken advantage of. I was hurt, angry, and confused. My entire world was turned upside down. My past, my current life, and my future were all called into question by one horrible act by my ex-wife.

I experienced very real depression for the first time in my life. My life, during and immediately after the divorce, was hell. I wouldn't wish that on my worst enemy.

Looking back on my early childhood, I never saw true romance or obvious lustfulness in my parents and their relationship. I didn't see it in my friends' parents, either. Later in life, I didn't see it in most of my adult friends and their marriages.

Everyone just acted like roommates with kids: two boring people going through the motions and running the family machine. When pressed, most of the men I knew would admit that they were not happy campers.

"The mass of men live lives of quiet desperation," said Henry David Thoreau.

I just figured this was the way marriage was supposed to be, ya know? Boring, but necessary. It's something we all go through in life, right? We learn that we need to temper our expectations and be grateful for what we have. Not everything has to be wine and roses. Sometimes you must ENDURE hardship for the greater good of the family and community.

Without marriage, I have been told again and again, our society would crumble. As far as my very real and normal sexual desires were concerned, I was led to believe they were waaaaay down the long list of "stuff that was important." I felt intense guilt for wanting more. I was told that just because you WANT something doesn't mean you get it. That's how life works.

Then I found out that my wife DID want the same things out of life. She wanted the same exciting relationship and the same level of sexuality and eroticism that I always wanted. She just didn't want that with me.

Ouch.

She filed for divorce immediately after the affair was discovered… And you know what? It was the best thing ever to happen to me.

I don't know what got into me, but after a brief trip down the well of depression, I went on one hell of a self-improvement kick. I just couldn't let this awful experience destroy me. I had three little ones looking to me as their oasis of normalcy. My youngest was only a year and a half old! Their mom was acting very strange and erratic; she spent less time with the kids as the months and years went by.

I've learned a lot about myself over these post-divorce years. I've learned I need a mission to keep my engine going. A purpose. I thrive on activity and can easily slip into lulls and use my busy home and work life as an excuse for avoiding the hard work of real self-improvement. I was good about going through the motions… but not really accomplishing anything.

Discovering the affair and experiencing the subsequent divorce was exactly the fuel I needed to get my engine going again. Finally… I had a mission.

I quickly learned that there are A LOT of guys out there just like me. I read a lot about the phenomenon and eventually, I wrote a lot about the topic, too (an old hobby of mine). It's therapeutic for me. I love to get my thoughts and energy on paper, so to speak. It allows me properly digest my thoughts and really SEE things from a different perspective.

I started a website at dadstartingover.com and eventually helpformen.com. Over the past eight years, my team of coaches and I have been blessed to help out thousands of men from all over the world. It's exhilarating to create something that so many men enjoy, but at the same time, it's sad that we're all united in our struggles.

The most popular topics on the Dad Starting Over and Help For Men websites, by far, are those related to dead bedrooms and cheating wives. It seems that men just aren't getting the sex they want, and they want to fix the situation. They NEED to fix it... and many come to our websites and buy our books after it's already too late.

I decided to write this book (now the THIRD edition of The Dead Bedroom Fix) not just to capitalize on the popularity of the topic, but also to get to the bottom of a common issue that can and will grow into something more insidious if it's not resolved early on.

A dead bedroom is, contrary to what your spouse and others may tell you, a very big freaking deal.

Half of all marriages end in divorce. It's a common statistic we're all familiar with. Second marriages have an even higher rate of divorce. What you may not know is that women initiate 70% of the divorces… and that number goes up to 80% if the woman is college-educated!

Women, in general, are not happy within the confines of a typical marriage. The phenomena of dead bedrooms and cheating wives reflect this.

Yes, I Married Again

As of this writing, my wife and I have been together for ten years. This is the second marriage for both of us, and we brought a new little girl into this world about three years ago.

So, given that a good decade has gone by AND we had a baby together… is this marriage really very different from my first marriage?

Oooooh yeah, it's different, alright.

We have lots of amazing sex. We have intimacy. We have romance. We love and respect each other a great deal. We are what you would call a "nauseating" couple. We have been this way, consistently, for over ten years.

This is my married life now. There is no alternative. If the sex life and intimacy go bye-bye, so does my commitment as her husband and partner and we will no longer be married.

Wow, that sounds really cold and blunt, doesn't it?
I'm cold and blunt because I know that without physical intimacy, there is no need for a monogamous relationship. None. I can get a roommate anywhere. I have friends. I can make more friends. I can get girlfriends. I can get meaningless sex. Been there, done that. It's not what I want out of life, but it's always an option.

The logistics, friendship, and comfort in our life together don't negate the need for real physical intimacy. You will never hear me say, *"The relationship is perfect… except for the sex."*

No sex = no relationship.

Don't misinterpret this as me saying, "She better give me sex, or else!" That's not at all what I'm saying. I'm saying that a lack of sex in a romantic relationship is indicative of much deeper issues that proliferate beyond the bedroom. As the author of this book, I know what it takes to "keep the spark alive" in my relationship. If my wife takes in all I have to offer and her response is, "Yeah… great, but I still don't want you," then I know we are done.

Simply put, not having sex is a sign of a very broken marriage. It's a sign that one or both of you have some very real emotional hangups that are NOT healthy.

You may still be a married couple, but you're no longer in a romantic relationship.

"Everything is great in our relationship… except for the sex," is the biggest bunch of bullshit ever uttered. It's right up there with "happy wife, happy life" (more on that later in this book).

I know what I want out of a committed, long-term monogamous relationship. I'm looking for something special in the woman I call "wife." I'm looking for a true partner in crime. I want somebody to experience wonderful and not-so-wonderful things with during my eighty-plus orbits around the sun. A good chunk of this life of mine revolves around sex. I don't hide this fact. I'm a dude, after all; I have the genitals to prove it.

So far, our intimacy as a couple is off the charts. I have volumes of dirty photos and videos that my WIFE has sent me over the years. We have a very sexy/kinky side to our lives that nobody else knows about. That is our little secret. To our friends, we are just a very sweet and loving couple that hugs and smooches a lot.

In my first marriage, I was a frequent "user" of porn, if you know what I mean. In my current marriage, porn is not a thing for ME to use as a coping mechanism, but rather a sexy tool that we sometimes use together. She enjoys doing these "dirty" things together as a couple. This is part of the secret, fun, and sexy side of our relationship that keeps us bonded together.

She has a body that most women at any age would kill for.

She has a naturally good shape, but she also works hard to keep it looking nice. I let her know I appreciate how sexy she is by banging the snot out of her, cuddling with her for hours, and showering her with praise and affection.

We are in a constant battle to keep in shape for each other. Yes, we sometimes let life get in the way and our sexiness slips a little here and there. With my genetics, I can put on ten pounds just by looking at a piece of cake. She then cranks up the yoga and cardio, sends me a sexy photo, I drool for hours… and the next day I hit the gym with just a little more oomph and lay off the carbs.

This is healthy and normal and not shallow and narcissistic, as some may claim. EFFORT is a key component in any marriage. The sexual component is just as important—if not MORE so—than every other component of the relationship. What about money? My wife has her own money. More than me, actually. She has a great career as a medical doctor. She doesn't need me to pay her bills or to buy her that nice purse she really wants. She needs me for physical/emotional intimacy and love. I'm not the provider of a paycheck; I provide in other ways.

I'm her rock. I'm her partner. I'm her man.

I must keep up the hard work and earn these relationship qualities. It can all go away tomorrow. I don't want to sign another round of divorce papers wondering, "What if…?" It's NOT easy, and that's the way it should be. As with anything in life, if it's worth it, it's going to take work.

I am crazy about the girl. That doesn't negate my own needs. My love and devotion are not unconditional.

For me, Dead Bedroom = Dead Marriage.

I'm never doing that again.

CHAPTER 1
DEAD BEDROOMS

"The great question that has never been answered and which I have not yet been able to answer, despite my thirty years of research into the feminine soul, is, 'What does a woman want?'"

—Sigmund Freud

What is a Dead Bedroom?

The "Dead Bedroom" is just what it sounds like: a monogamous romantic relationship with little to no sexual activity between the two partners.

For the purposes of this book and its intended audience, we will stick with the tried-and-true trope of the horny husband and the cold, disinterested wife. As any therapist or psychologist will tell you, more often than not it's the woman who is the "low libido" partner in a marriage.

It's a well-known cultural meme and has been for a long, long time.

"Marriage is a lot like prison, but without the sex." — Anonymous

"Married sex is like being awake during your own autopsy. It is root canal work without anesthetic." — Al Goldstein

"I know nothing about sex because I was always married." — Zsa Zsa Gabor

"Sex is the most beautiful thing that can take place between a happily married man and his secretary." — Barry Humphries

These stereotypes didn't just fall from the sky. The dead bedroom happens, and it happens a lot in long-term, monogamous relationships. In fact, I've often said that drifting apart sexually seems to be our default programming as human beings. We pair-bond, we are hyper-sexual, we procreate, we make sure the new little one is alive and safe… and then we slowly drift apart. Our job as the baby-making human male is over.

You've seen this dynamic played out again and again on television and in the movies. You see it with your friends and their relationships. You probably saw it with your parents and extended family.

You think back on your childhood and remember yourself as a little boy, sitting at the dinner table on Thanksgiving Day. Dad is cutting the turkey and says something about the "juicy breast" and gives your mom a playful smile and a wink. You weren't quite sure what was going on, but his energy made you smile and laugh.

But then… your mom's tone changes instantly. She gives him an angry look and says "Seriously?" as she lets out a frustrated sigh and shoves another forkful of food in her face. Dad doesn't take it well. He pouts the rest of the day and ignores everyone while watching football.

The negativity in the house is palpable.

Fast forward to now and your relationship with your wife. You come home after a long day at the office. The commute was extra annoying, and you just want to put your feet up and relax… but you can't. You immediately tend to the kids, help with dinner, take out the trash, answer some work emails, help your son with homework, play teatime with your daughter, and then help put everyone to bed. Finally, after three bedtime stories, your job is done, and it is time to relax.

You plop in bed next to your wife. She's wearing sweatpants and a stained T-shirt. Not very sexy, but you're a man and it's been a while since you last had sexual release (beyond your usual porn/masturbation sessions). You make your typical sexy growl sound that you think is so funny, playfully squint your eyes, smile, and move your hand to her breast.

She immediately grabs your hand and pushes it away.

"Seriously? Can you just give it a rest for one night?"

She rolls over and turns off the light.

You would be mad or confused if this was a new thing. Instead, you're just sad. Defeated. This is normal for your marriage and has been for a while.

She says, "Give it a rest for one night," but it's been two months since you had any kind of physical intimacy. No long kisses. No loving back rubs. No holding hands while walking through the neighborhood. No random make-out sessions on the couch. No sex.

Nothing.

She holds the master key to your sex life and the door is locked. It has been locked for way too long.

As a son, husband, and father, the message is clear: The man is a horny, out-of-control bag of testosterone that needs to be put in his place.

His energy must be redirected towards the more important tasks, like providing for the family, helping with chores, and letting his wife get much-needed rest. If he doesn't leave her alone, there is hell to pay.

The woman is the cold, bossy, and domineering presence in the home. She keeps things on track and must occasionally swat away his attempts to bring sexuality into their world. "No! Bad dog!"

When Dad veers off the assigned path, he must be punished and reminded of his primary and preferred role as the provider. Mom will not hesitate to say or do something that will emasculate him and make him feel like a pervert for introducing sexuality into their relationship. It's not about hurting his feelings. It's about stopping his annoying and inappropriate behavior.

As a result, Dad will act like a baby for a while. He'll eventually get over it and then the process will start all over again. Rinse and repeat.

Sound familiar?

Maybe your situation isn't THIS bad, but you ARE reading this book right now which means one thing is certain: You sure aren't happy with your sex life. This has GOT to change and the sooner the better.

What Caused YOUR Dead Bedroom?

You are not alone

On my websites at dadstartingover.com and helpformen.com, as well as our various social media channels, I have written dozens of articles and put out hundreds of videos on a variety of relationship and self-improvement topics. By far, my most popular topics are Dead Bedrooms and Female Infidelity. The same goes for my podcast. Any episode related to "Dead Bedrooms" is way ahead of any other episode.

On the popular website www.talkaboutmarriage.com, the two most active "focused" topics are "Sex in Marriage" and "Coping With Infidelity."

On the popular website Reddit.com, the DeadBedrooms forum (subreddit) has over 450,000 subscribers.

People sure do seem to have issues with sex and marriage. I mean, it's not surprising, is it? It can be argued that the modern-day version of the traditional marriage goes against our basic and animalistic nature. Today's marriage tells men:

> *"You know that urge you have to bang every pretty woman you see? Stop that. Here's your one woman for the rest of your life. You'll love her and want her, but she may or may not want to have sex with you… probably not most of the*

time… and there's really nothing you can do about it. So… have fun!"

At the same time, marriage tells women:

"I know you dream of finding the all-around best guy for you to settle down with and make babies. Good luck with that! You're not worthy of 'winning' such a guy, so here's some boring schmuck who is about as far from your ideal lover as you can get. But… don't worry. He will provide for you and your children and will love you a great deal. The good news is that you don't have to have sex with him. He'll still take care of you, regardless. You'll probably end up loathing him. Enjoy!"

Marriage doesn't have to be this way… but more often than not, it sure does seem to go in that direction.

The no-bullshit truth is that your wife, within your relationship… with YOU… is not experiencing sexual desire.

If she were experiencing sexual desire, you would know it. You wouldn't be Googling "wife doesn't want sex" at midnight while she snores next to you in bed. Instead, you would be covered in sweat and sleeping with a smile on your face.

Instead of asking, "Why am I in a dead bedroom?" you should instead ask, "Why is my wife no longer experiencing sexual desire for me?" That's when you start to get down to the actual cause of your problem.

The dead bedroom is most likely the result of a series of negative actions or inactions on the part of the man. The man was presented with all the typical obstacles that get in the way of sex (kids, stress, time, familiarity, bored wife) and he didn't respond in the correct way. These actions and inactions over the years never properly pushed the buttons his wife needed to be pushed to activate her sex drive (especially after parenthood).

You did X and you got Y in return. It's that simple.

Yep, I just put the responsibility for this situation squarely on your shoulders. Kinda shitty and presumptuous of me, right? Yes, it is. But, there's good reason for me to come to this conclusion.

I've heard thousands of dead bedroom stories from men, and after much back-and-forth, soul-searching, and honest reflection, they always come to the same conclusion: They royally messed up somewhere along the way. They either erroneously stayed with the absolute WORST partner imaginable—I hear this far too often… many men I talk to suffer from emotional and physical abuse at the hands of their wives—or he actually married a really good woman who naturally responded to her husband's mistakes in a very predictable way: She lost attraction to him and her sexual desire dwindled down to nothing.

Either way, the man had a series of "fork in the road"

moments during his relationship, and he continuously chose the wrong path.

Your situation could be different than everyone else's, but I sincerely doubt it.

The good news is that YOU probably caused this, so YOU can probably fix it.

You're a dude. You like to fix things, right? That's why you're reading this book. You want to find out what part of the relationship machine broke down and caused it to stop working and spill oil all over the garage floor.

Make no mistake about it, your relationship is broken. Sex is not just one tiny aspect of an overall awesome relationship (like many "low-libido" wives will tell their husbands). It's the biggest part.

Without sex, you are just roommates.

Without sex, you are not fulfilling your most basic, normal, healthy human need.

Without sex, you will experience a cascading series of events that will ultimately lead to a lesser version of yourself and the end of your marriage.

If the relationship machine is not maintained properly, it will break down. If you put the wrong kind of oil in, the motor will seize up. You'll be left on the side of the road, scratching your head and wondering what to do next. Unfortunately, relationships don't come with an owner's manual. We received numerous textbooks in school, but none of them were titled, How to Be the Kind of Man Your Wife Will Want to Fuck For Many Years.

But, for some strange reason, men all sure seem to act like this non-existent book of rules really DOES exist.

This mystery book is packed with libido-igniting nuggets of wisdom like:

1. **Buy her gifts.** Flowers. Chocolates. Massages. Make her feel appreciated. You can purchase affection.

2. **Do more chores.** Take the stress away from her life. Watching you do work around the house will turn her on.

3. **Happy wife, happy life!** Be more agreeable. Less drama and less stress are a good thing. The more you agree with her and just go along with whatever she wants, the more she will have sex with you.

4. **Pretend that no other females in the world exist.** Your focus should be solely on your wife. Temper your sexual urges. If she sees that you are a eunuch when it comes to other women, she will be turned on and want to have more sex with you.

5. **Talk to her.** Make sure she really understands the problem and sees things from your point of view. Appeal to

her rational side. Open up to her emotionally. The more she rationally understands your need for sex, the more turned on she will be.

In theory, they all sound great. You're more giving, you're a better housekeeper, you're more agreeable, you're more open with your feelings, and you're more devoted. What's not to like?

What's funny is that every one of these is the exact opposite of what men should do when the sex goes south. In fact, they are the continuation and amplification of what caused your dead bedroom in the first place.

That's right, if we want to look at the CAUSE of the dead bedroom, we just need to look at what men typically do to try and fix it. It's the same damn thing.
How ironic.

Let's look at each of the five solutions that men try again and again. Let's break down just how and why each fails so miserably… and why we continue trying anyway.

CHAPTER 2
THE COMMON MISTAKES

"For things to reveal themselves to us, we need to be ready to abandon our views about them."

—Thich Nhat Hanh

Mistake #1: Gift Giving

We all know the tried-and-true stereotype of the nervous guy showing up to the first date with flowers. Maybe he takes it up a notch and adds a box of chocolates. The chocolates may be reserved for Valentine's Day, but he will for sure keep buying gifts throughout their first date. He will buy drinks. Dinner. Maybe a little stuffed teddy bear. "Awww!" she says throughout the night.

What's he saying with all this gift-giving?

> *"Ok, here's the deal. You just sit there and look good, and I'll give you free stuff. Sound like a plan? No, I don't expect anything from you. You don't have to qualify yourself. Your vagina and the possibility of one day being inside of it is more than enough for me. Here, let me buy you something else so you don't forget how good I am."*

If for some reason, the flowers and constant gift-giving results in a girlfriend, then the conditioning has been imprinted on the man.

Gift-giving = Affection from women.

What if he had NOT bought things for her right up front? What if he expected her to chip in for everything or that, God forbid, SHE should pay for dinner? Would she go on a second date and eventually marry him? No, probably not. She would tell you the same thing. She liked that he was so generous; it made her feel special.

So, what does that tell you?

He bought her affection.

Does that bode well for long-term romantic love? Maybe… maybe not. But, that sure does seem to be the standard courtship-process template for much of the world.

The man demonstrates that he has resources and the ability to procure more. This shows that he can take care of the woman and subsequent babies they may one day make together. This proves to the woman that he is worthy of more dates.

(As you will learn in this book and other similar material, this whole "mating game" is, in fact, one giant silly animalistic exercise.)

Maybe you have convinced yourself that your wife has EARNED the gifts that you give to her. Even though she doesn't seem to have any attraction towards you and treats you like a nuisance, she IS your wife. That is, in itself, worthy of praise, right?

Let's be honest: You're rewarding your wife for simply being the female in the relationship. If we examine this further, it's also a subtle form of sexism. You're putting her up on a pedestal just because she has boobies and a hoohah.
You're being creepy.

This is the pathetic theme of your gift-giving:

*"I don't get much in the way of sex… and we all know you
don't like me all that much… so I need to bribe you to keep
you around. I'll take whatever crumbs I can get. Please,
don't leave me. My sexual options in life are so dismal that
I'm willing to pay for the slim chance of eventually sleeping
with you one day."*

Guess what? She's fully aware of the dynamic at play here.
She knows she has you by the marbles and she will drag
this relationship on as long as possible to extract as many
resources from you as she can.

This is not evil. This is human nature.

Young girls get their homework done for them and a free
ride to the mall. Women get free flowers, meals, drinks, a
shoulder to cry on, and later… a doting husband.

What do men not get in return? Great sex. More specifically,
they don't get a woman who finds them sexually attractive.
It never works out in the end. Ever.

What the gift-giving does is put you right away in the mode
of the "Provider."

The Provider readily gives up his resources: time, money,
and commitment. He does so out of an instinctual male
need to make sure his family is safe and secure… and out of
the thinly veiled hope of getting the pretty lady to have sex
with him.

When taken to the extreme, especially with little to no reward in return, it's seen as extremely NEEDY behavior. It's a giant advertisement for the inherent scarcity the man feels when it comes to something as important as finding and keeping a sexual mate.

The Provider sees his consistent GIVING as a positive personality trait that puts him above those in the shallow Lover category. (I'll cover more about the Lover/Provider dynamic later.) He will NEVER admit that his good deeds are anything but 100% altruistic. He's doing his manly duty, after all. This is expected of him and has been hammered into his head from an early age.

A man wins the love and affection of a woman. A shortcut method to win such affection is to buy her things. If he were being honest, he would admit that he gave and gave for the purpose of getting something in return.

The truth is, he just wants love and affection, and giving is his way of trying to earn those rewards. When it doesn't work out, he gets pissed. When he emotes to others about his relationship problems, the first thing he brings up is all the things he bought for her:

- *"But…I bought her flowers last week!"*
- *"But…I got her that bracelet last month!"*
- *"But… I paid for that house cleaning service she wanted!"*

The message from the man is clear:

"I'm a very needy guy. I NEED my wife and her affection. The understood deal between us is that I do nice things for her, and she's SUPPOSED to reward me with physical affection."

Unbeknownst to the husband, what does this gift-giving subconsciously tell his wife?

"Being a cold and disinterested wife gets my husband to take action and buy stuff that I want. Yes, he's pitiful and I lost respect for him years ago, but at least I get stuff out of it. I like stuff. I better keep treating him like dirt. This is working."

Human Psych 101: Reward a certain behavior and you'll get more of it. It's all about conditioning. Much like Pavlov's dog, we're easily trained animals.

The husband is conditioned to believe, from a young age, that gift-giving results in the romantic relationship he wants. This continues into adulthood and becomes a fall-back "fixer" strategy for when things start to go bad. This is an absolute no-win situation.

Gift-giving should always come from a genuine place with no ulterior motive. It should come from the mindset of rewarding somebody for being a good person. You should never expect anything in return. You do this because you love and appreciate your partner… not because you want more blowjobs.

Do you really love and appreciate your wife when she emasculates you and shames you for still wanting her after all these years?

No.

Then why reward her? Because you hope to turn her attitude around.

By giving gifts, you are simply doubling down on your Provider role in an underhanded way. Your gifts are not genuine. She innately knows this.

You're being manipulative. You're being creepy. You're being needy. You're being pathetic.
Provider = Comfort and safety. Comfort does not necessarily equal sexual attraction (more on this later).

Provider with an ulterior motive = Creepy and needy.

Creepy and needy equals revulsion.

You're actively pushing her away, and you're wondering why the distance between you two continues to grow.

There's no way to win here. Cut it out.

Mistake #2: Chore Play

There is nothing special about doing household chores. They must get done. Having a penis doesn't give you a "get-out-of-doing-chores" card, as many men in some parts of the world still believe. If the sink is full of dishes, you put them in the dishwasher. If the trash is full, you take it out. You make the bed. It's not rocket science. It's not difficult.

Contrary to popular belief, doing household chores is not tough. It's annoying and sometimes time-consuming, but it's not difficult. Building a bridge or drilling for oil is physically demanding and requires a lot of brainpower to do correctly. Pulling a sheet over a mattress is something a seventy-year-old grandma with crippling arthritis can do.

So why do I list doing more chores as a "mistake" if I seem so adamant about doing them? Well, the problem comes when you do these much-needed household chores and proudly bring it up to mommy… err… your wife:

"Honey, I put away the dishes for you!!"

Well whoopty-fucking-doo, little man. Welcome to adulthood. Want a cookie?

No, you want love and affection. It's obvious.

It's extremely needy behavior. It's a giant turnoff.

This, my friends, is "choreplay."

Running a household takes work. Not all that work is manly or intellectually stimulating. Some of it involves things like cleaning the cat box and folding laundry. If you see it needs to be done and you have time to do it, you do it. That's called being an adult. That's what we all do.

By bragging about it or doing it with a future reward in mind, you're lowering yourself to a sub-adult level. My youngest child used to love to show me how he cleaned up a mess (he usually just made it worse). He wanted to impress me and show me that he was a big boy now. He needed my approval.

That's precisely what you are doing. You're not getting sex, so you bump up your housework in an effort to gain approval from your wife.

You are acting like a child. You're being very needy. Your wife doesn't want to fuck a needy child. She wants a man. She wants the kind of guy who does the annoying and time-consuming tasks and never brings it up. She wants a scenario like this:

Her: *"Wait… did you fix the lamp, fold the laundry, AND clean that stain on the carpet?"*

You: *"Ummm… yeah?"*

Her: *"When did you find time to do that?!"*

You: *"I dunno… last night, I think."*

Her: *"Thank you, baby!! I just noticed. That is so awesome."*

You: *"No problem, sweet cheeks."*

That sound like a positive exchange? That sound like something an adult MAN would do? Of course. He just did the work and never mentioned it. It had to get done. He really didn't give a shit if she approved or not. That's not the purpose of the work. The purpose of the work was to alleviate the issue of the annoying flickering lamp, the giant pile of clothes, and the carpet that had an annoying yogurt stain on it.

There were problems; he fixed them. Simple as that. No big deal. Certainly nothing you do to win sexual intimacy or attention from your wife. To try and equate the world of housework with the frequency of sex is not a good thing. So then, why do so many men fall back on doing additional chores to try and reignite their wife's sex drive?

Because, as I said before, men are FIXERS.

Sex life broken? Well then, let's get to patching up these holes and get this sex boat floating again!

Step one: LISTEN to the wife for guidance. Does she complain? Well, yeah. Of course. She's a woman. If she's breathing, she's complaining, right?

What exactly is she complaining about the most?

She is very TIRED. This seems to be the overall theme of her day-to-day existence. She's constantly worn out. She's overwhelmed to the point of exhaustion. The kids. The job. The house. She will usually point to this extreme exhaustion as the primary cause for her lack of libido.

Well, you can't make the kids go away and you can't make her job at the office any easier… but you CAN do more housework for her! That's it, then. That's the new fixer strategy. Do more housework. Yes, this is genius.

In fact, many a man has reported that his wife, after he complained for the seventeenth time about the lack of sex in their marriage, specifically said that his helping more around the house would ignite her sexual desire.

"Maybe if you did more house stuff to help me out…" many men have heard.

So, when she comes home, you will point out that you did the dishes, folded the laundry, and cleaned the cat litter box. She will jump for joy, collapse into your arms, and then promptly rip her clothes off and rediscover that sex drive of hers that went missing for so long… right?!

Yeah, no. It doesn't work that way. Sexual desire is a little more complicated than that.

See… again… you're doing things because you want to get something out of it. You can try to convince yourself that you're just being a good partner, but we both know that's bullshit.

If your wife sat you down and said, "Honey… look, no matter what you do or say, we are never having sex again. Ever. EVER. Got it?!" you would be camped out in the garage pouting all day. Chores wouldn't even be on the radar.

You're doing things for mommy's approval. It's obvious. It's needy. It's weak.

Chores are like taking a shit: It's not the sexiest, most awesome thing in the world to do… but you do it anyway. It must get done. You don't care what she thinks about it. That would be weird.

You just do it.

You're a big boy. The time of getting rewarded for going potty stopped decades ago.

Mistake #3: Happy Wife, Happy LIfe

Wow, if I had a nickel for every time I've heard this stupid phrase.

In fact, I can think of one particular memory from seven years ago. It involved myself, my kids, my wife, and some random shoe store employee.

We needed shoes for my oldest boy. (He was ten at the time.) We had an event coming up and he needed something nice but not too formal. He had grown out of everything he had at home (like kids always seem to do)… so off to the mall we went!

We went to Macy's and decided to split up. My wife went to look at some dresses and my son and I went to the shoe department. We tried on a few pairs and found one we both liked, but I wasn't sure about them and wanted my wife's input.

For one thing, I'm color-blind. Sometimes I don't see obvious color mismatches that make everyone else laugh uncontrollably. I honestly didn't know if those shoes would go with the outfit that we already bought for our son.

Second, I can't trust my son to pick out something color-wise because, well, he was a ten-year-old boy at the time… and that means he had the fashion sense of a crazy man with a bad cocaine habit.

The wife eventually wrapped up her dress shopping and met us at the shoe department. We showed her the one pair we both liked. She liked them, too… but, she didn't think it went too well with the outfit we bought for him. The shoelaces were a little too funky looking. Overall, the shoes were too sneaker-like, in her opinion. The style really limited what clothes he could wear with them.

Good point. We continued looking.

We walked into another shoe store and my wife grabbed a pair off the shelf. "Here, these are much better." My son and I looked at the shoes and blurted out at the same time, *"They look JUST like the other pair!"*

She sighed and pointed out that no, they were not JUST like the other pair. Those had plain laces and not those speckled, funny-looking laces the other pair had. Overall, they were more formal-looking. They looked a little more sedate and would therefore have had more options for matching clothes.

Ten seconds into our conversation, the guy running the shoe store loudly said in our direction, *"Dude! Let me give you a hint! HAPPY WIFE, HAPPY LIFE!!"*

The message was simple:

   "Noooo! Don't have conflict with a woman! Let her win!

Live another day, you poor man!"

How pathetic. After one very mild and normal exchange between my wife and me, this random shoe store worker was ready to throw in the towel for me. He was so unnerved by the site of a man disagreeing with a woman that he had to come to my rescue. I can just picture him grabbing me by the hand and looking sullenly into my eyes like a wise old man telling the hero of a movie not to battle the evil Medusa:

"Oh… you poor, poor man. Don't you realize what evil you are up against? Please… for your own sake, go back from where you came. You are not prepared for this battle."

What in the Sam Hill happened to men? Why are we all so conflict averse? Are we really that frightened of women? That's what we're saying after all, right… that we're legitimately afraid of them?

We're so afraid of women that many of us can't point out when we disagree with something. We let anger and resentment fester and turn into cancer and heart disease because… you don't want to make a scene? You don't want to make her mad?

Seriously?

"Yes, dear." Another common relationship trope. The resigned man. The droopy face. The slumped shoulders. The attitude that says, *"I don't care. Do whatever you like. Just*

stop making me so anxious, okay? Please?"

It's defeat. It's passivity. It's pathetic. It's a GIANT turnoff. You think you're just being an adult and keeping the waters calm. You don't want to rock the boat unnecessarily. You are, what the experts call, "conflict averse." Your wife is far more emotional than you are, and you don't want to disrupt the current state of calm.

As many men can attest, we just want PEACE. But, with your wife, one little thing can set her off… and goodbye peace and quiet. You've learned this over the years. When she does go off, she's a real handful. It's unattractive, annoying, brings about a great deal of anxiety in you, and it makes you question the relationship. You'd prefer not to go there if you can help it.

You just want everyone to be happy.

"Sigh… That's fine, honey."

What does she think of this reaction from you? Well, sure, she's happy at first. She gets her way. She's elated. Like a small child, she will say "Yaaaay!" and bounce around for a little while.

Over time, getting her way is just expected. The novelty is gone. Soon she won't even ask for your opinion on anything. She'll just do what she wants. She knows you wouldn't object anyway, so why delay the inevitable?

More importantly, one big thing happens: She loses respect for you.

If she doesn't respect you, she's not fucking you.

When you try to avoid drama, what you're really trying to avoid is your own anxiety. She makes you feel bad. Your emotional state should not be so fragile and pliable. You do your thing and let her emote. If her emotions cross the line and she is disrespectful to you, you let her know immediately:

"You're being an asshole. Stop it. Now."

Believe it or not, she wants to be told NO every now and then. Sometimes she really does want to be told to sit down, shut her mouth, and stop acting like such a spoiled brat. You are a man. You are supposed to be a rock. You are supposed to be dependable. Sometimes that means welcoming confrontation and dealing with bullshit; sometimes that bullshit comes from your own wife.

Doing the opposite, being a spineless pushover people-pleaser, elicits a feeling of disrespect, uncertainty, and disdain from her. That is NOT good for the female sex drive.

"So, wait… she doesn't like it when I submit and say, 'Yes, dear' for the 500th time, but she'll also throw a huge fit if she doesn't get her way. Seriously? Why would she do this? I can't win!"

— Every guy who ever lived.

To try and help explain, a lot of men have concluded that this "bad" behavior from their wife is a type of test. You'll often hear them called "shit tests" or "fitness tests." Their purpose, as many men believe, is to throw out something negative and then sit back and watch how you handle it. A sneaky way of saying:

"Show me what you got, big boy."

She's testing your boundaries. She wants to see what you're REALLY made of. I've even heard some women flat-out admit to consciously doing it.

Everyone, no matter what their gender, tests other people. We all do this consciously and subconsciously, and your wife is no different.

Your boss will test you by asking you to come in and work over the weekend… but he can't pay you overtime. You better believe that if you say yes, he will expect the same pushover attitude from here on out.

Your friend who has never lifted a finger to help you with anything asks you to help him move into his new house. If you say yes, you have trained him to think that he can continue taking advantage of your friendship… and you better believe he will.

As your spouse, your wife's tests are a way of seeing just

how strong a partner you really are. If you cave in to her demands, never stand up for yourself, refuse to make a decision, or freak out and pout after every little verbal tirade she has, what does that say about you?

"He can't deal with ME? Well, then how the hell can he deal with the tough stuff in life? How can he protect me and the family? What kind of man is this?"

The result? Her innate programming sends signals to her body: "This male is weak. Do not copulate. His genes are not fit for mating. He will produce sub-standard babies." The result? No sexy time for you.

Remember… if she doesn't respect you, she's not fucking you.

What you are doing by saying, *"Yes, dear,"* for the hundredth time is being "agreeable." Agreeableness is a personality trait that is most often seen in women. Women are more apt to be amicable, trusting, and compliant.

In other words, they are usually more submissive than men. Not always, of course, but usually.

When you just go with the flow and comply and submit to her every whim, you are being submissive. You are, in essence, acting like a woman.

She doesn't want a woman. She wants a man.
Again… if she doesn't respect you, she's not fucking you.

Mistake #4: Pretend That No Other Females in the World Exist

If you're a man and you're healthy and everything is functioning as it should be, you probably have a relatively strong libido. You want to have sex. A lot. A lot more than what you are having right now. Obviously… or you wouldn't be reading this.

It's a biological fact that you have evolved to procreate with a lot of different women. Monogamy does seem to be the relationship norm throughout the world, regardless of religious affiliation or socio-economic status. BUT, it is an observed trait in men that we choose to have multiple mates if we have the opportunity to do so. In fact, we know from DNA data and from studying history that polygyny—the act of mating with more than one woman—is the mating habit of choice for men… IF the man has the power and resources to attract and retain multiple mates.

In other words, if men have the choice to do so (via their looks, wealth, power, and opportunity), they'll bang more than one woman during their lifetime.

"Men are only as faithful as their options." — Chris Rock

As a man, you have about ten times the amount of testosterone that your wife has. Testosterone is the hormone that largely determines libido in human beings. Before you email me, yes, I realize human biology and psychology are not that simple and way more goes into sex drive than just one hormone… but try taking a shot of testosterone every week for a month and get back to me on how it affects you (hint: you're probably going to be WAY hornier). I can remember reading the reaction of a woman who was prescribed testosterone therapy by her doctor: *"This is crazy. I can't live like this. All I think about is sex."*

As you read this, you are making sperm. Millions of them. Those little guys need to come out and they need to make babies to keep our species going. Mother Nature made sure you do your part by imprinting you with basic programming that pushes you to do your job and to do it often.

This is the programming that makes you look at all those pretty young women at the mall. Repeatedly.

This is the programming that makes you keep looking at that MILF in the PTO meeting who just got the new boob implants.

This is the programming that makes pornography a billion-dollar industry.

This is the programming that makes prostitution "the world's oldest profession."

Our sex drive is an essential part of who we are as men. It's THERE, and we live with it. It's natural. It's not going away.

It's a big part of what makes us men.

Guess what? Your wife knows ALL about your strong sex drive. She knows you masturbate to porn. She knows you fantasize. She caught you checking out that young lady the other day at the beach. She probably said something about it. Depending on the health of your relationship, she may have even shamed you for it.

Men erroneously believe that once they are married, this drive and attraction to others must be hidden away. We think of ourselves as stupid, horny animals. It seems that our community requires that we keep these urges at bay and channel that energy into our role as a family provider. To do otherwise means that we are encroaching on "asshole" territory, or worse, "unfit husband and dad."

So… how in the hell is your ever-present and much-maligned male sexuality supposed to fit into the preferred "Provider" role?

It's very confusing and very frustrating.

Regardless of what society may tell us, these urges we have must come out, one way or another. If not, we lose our minds.

But wait a minute… what is this?? We have a woman in the house!? Our wife! Yes, of course! We love her! We even married her! Sweet! Let's get this show on the road.

You: *"Honey! Let's have sex! It will be awesome!"*

Her: *"No."*

You: *"God dammit."*

Now what? Well, if you're like most men out there, you know all the major video-streaming porn websites by heart. You probably have a favorite category of video you like and a favorite "actress." Probably a few specific links you bookmarked. They seem to always get the job done in a hurry.

Then your wife sees your internet browser history. She doesn't like it. You're not supposed to like those things anymore, remember? Did you forget your role in life? What kind of man and father are you? Why are you watching this stuff? Cut it out already, you sicko pervert.

You have been shamed for your sexuality. This seems to be the go-to strategy for many women who want to quickly cut off the husband's journey towards expressing his sexual desire.

Pornography, sex workers… even staring at another human for a brief second… all are evil and shameful. The ultimate irony is the person doing the shaming is the one you physically want so much… yet she is frustratingly off-limits. In essence, your wife is saying, "No, you can't express your sexuality towards people outside of this relationship. Oh, and no, I don't want you sexually, either."

What the hell can you do!?

You know what to do! You'll take things up a notch. You feel that she probably doubts your attraction to her and questions your faithfulness. You'll show her that she's dead wrong. In fact, you don't NEED all that outside stimuli anymore. You'll show her how devoted you are to her and only her!

You'll show her your softer, more romantic side! She likes that!

You'll show her that no other woman on the planet exists but HER!

Then she will realize what a romantic you really are, she'll remember why she fell in love with you, and your sex life will be reignited.

Yeah… no.

Just like with your fear of confrontation (happy wife, happy life), you are pretending. You are withholding your true feelings, your true NATURE, with the underhanded purpose of getting affection from your wife.

This is not good.

She knows what you're really all about. She's been aware of the true sexual nature of men since she went into puberty and suddenly sprouted boobs. She's seen the creepy stares from older men, or worse…

She knows you have urges. You've probably reminded her of your needs on numerous occasions. She's well aware of your condition as a human male.

By tempering these urges and professing that SHE ALONE holds the key to your manly human nature (with or without actual sex from her), you are putting her right up on a pedestal. Again.

She has no option but to look down on you.

Remember, if she doesn't respect you, she's not fucking you. Here's a very common relationship "shit test" scenario:

You and your wife are watching TV. It's one of those "Bachelor" reality shows where the hunky lover guy gets to go on dates and pick from a harem of attractive women. One will eventually be chosen, and the lucky girl gets to be his girlfriend or even fiancée.

It's woman porn, basically.

Wife: *"Which girl do you think looks the best?"*

Husband: *"Oh, I dunno."*

Wife: *"No, tell me. Which one would you pick if you were him? Be honest."*

Husband (sweating profusely): "*Ummm... well... the blond one looks a lot like you. You have better legs, though.*"

Wife: "*Ha! You're so full of shit. She's like TWENTY years old and is flawless. She's an Olympic track athlete! I've never had legs like that. I haven't been to the gym in like fifteen years.*"

Husband: "*Oh, well, I think you're beautiful the way you are.*"

Wife: "*The way I am? What the hell is that supposed to mean? How AM I, exactly?*"

Husband: "*Sigh...*"

Test FAILED.

As you can see in this scenario, even the well-intentioned lie backfires. She sniffed out his bullshit right away. She knows he finds those women attractive and she knows she's no spring chicken anymore. Instead of being honest, the man starts mumbling and spazzing out like some nerdy teenager getting caught jerking off in the bathroom.

Admitting your attraction to others is not shameful. You haven't been "caught" doing something bad. Take pride in your sexuality.

Here's how that conversation would go between my wife and I:

Wife: *"Which girl do you think looks the best?"*

Me: *"Hmmmm… I like the brunette. There's something sexy about her. She has a nice body but looks a little rough around the edges. I bet she's kinky, though. The redhead is a little chubby but pretty. She has that girl-next-door look. Hmmmm… tough decision. Probably the brunette."*

Wife: *"Yeah, but the brunette is just a few years away from looking really rough. Kinda crazy, too. Not good wife material. I like the blond."*

Me: *"Oh, I wasn't thinking wife material. I'm thinking of just a few hours of fun. She would get annoying really fast. She's nuttier than squirrel poop."*

Wife: *"Haha! Yep."*

See the difference? It's light-hearted, honest, and playful. It's fun but sexy talk.

Ok, but what if a husband was being honest and it backfired on him?

Wife: *"You know what… you're an asshole. If you had asked me about a bunch of guys, I would say none of them looked good. I don't care about other men. Apparently, you care about other women a whole lot."*

Husband: *"HA! No, ya big dummy. You asked me, I'm gonna tell ya. The brunette is hot."*

Wife: "Whatever."

Wife is pissed. Wife pouts.

The strong, honest, and attractive husband doesn't care. He thinks it's hilarious. Why should he take this seriously? He answered her silly question. If she was fishing for comfort and lies instead of truth, she could go talk to her girlfriends. Her man is a rock and is there to be honest. She can count on him to be truthful, even when it hurts a little. Especially about a silly thing like which girl is the prettiest on a TV reality show.

The moment will blow over. It's no big deal. Breathe in, breathe out. No big deal.

"Which girl do you think looks the best?" = "Are you willing to be honest with me and with yourself even if it means hurting my feelings? Can you handle the possible nagging and anger that will result, or will you fold like a little baby?"

Remember: If a man can't be true to himself, he can't be true to others. He's untrustworthy. He's a slimy wuss. You always want to err on the side of integrity and honesty. Always. This goes for all facets of life, not just your romantic relationships.

A wife knows that her man is a sexual creature. She knows he's attracted to other women. A LOT of other women. He wants to have sex with them. Duh. He's a man. He doesn't go out and fornicate with a bunch of women because he is married and devoted to his wife. He is making a sacrifice. She knows it. You know it. Stop changing reality to accommodate her feelings. Stop tiptoeing around her. Stop walking on eggshells. It's okay if she's pissed off; it's not the end of the world.

Want to gauge just how sexually attracted your wife is to you? Have somebody ask her:

> *"How quickly do you think your husband could get another woman and have sex with her?"*

Does she laugh? That means you're not a sexual being in her eyes. You're a Provider that she lost respect for and no longer sees as a sexually viable creature. You have a lot of work ahead of you.

Does she get worried or angry at the idea? She knows you're attractive and a good catch. Your resources and partnership could easily go bye-bye.

Does she get turned on? Well then, what the hell are you doing reading this book? She's a horn dog and is crazy about you!

The man who other women find attractive is attractive to his wife. The man who could go out and get sex next week is a guy who is frequently banging his wife.

"He could have a lot of other pretty women, but he chose me."

This is rare in a husband these days. Rare is good. That's your goal. A big part of reaching that goal is being a strong man of integrity.

Mistake #5: Talk, Talk, Talk, Talk

Alright, you've tried romantic gifts of appreciation, you've upped your chore game, you're much more agreeable, and you've reassured her that there is no other woman that even comes remotely close to turning you on like she does. Didn't work, did it? Your sex life seems to be stuck on "terrible." No passion. No oomph. At best, your wife is giving you pity sex to shut you up: "Sigh… fine. We have ten minutes. Be quiet, I don't want the kids to wake up."

Now what do you do? Call it quits? Leave her? Find somebody new?

Well, again… you're a man. You're not done tinkering around under the hood of the car. You're determined to figure out why this engine is misfiring so badly. Where's the damn oil leak coming from?!

You ask around for advice. Maybe you have a close friend or two you can talk to about this kind of stuff. If you're like a lot of guys I talk to, you don't have such a friendship, so you go to the internet. You watch YouTube videos. You read books. You listen to podcasts.

One thing is repeated again and again by everyone:

COMMUNICATION. Everything is solved by effective communication.

When you feel a certain way, you should just tell your spouse, right? Makes sense. That's what adults are supposed to do. We get our issues out in the open and talk about them until they are resolved. Give and take. Compromise. This is part of any good partnership.

You want sex. It's important to you. She obviously doesn't feel the same way. Maybe this is the natural state for a wife/mom to be in, and you just need to remind her that couples are supposed to have sex. Maybe she just legitimately forgets about the importance of physical intimacy.

Maybe she doesn't understand just HOW important this is to you. Maybe if you sit her down and nicely explain how hurt you are by this lack of intimacy, she will suddenly comply and start her sexual engine up again for you. Ultimately, physical intimacy is a choice, right?

So, if you're like most men, you eventually cave in to your frustration and tell her how you feel. She listens. She gets a little emotional as you pour your guts out to her. You find yourself getting emotional and you describe the feelings you have every time she ignores you or flat-out rejects you so much. She seems genuinely surprised that you were so hurt by this. She says you have sex at least once every couple of weeks… isn't that enough? You explain to her that you started keeping track of sex and it's been two months since your last session. Before that, there was a three-month break. She seems puzzled by this. *Are you sure it's been that long?"*

Obviously, this sexual drought doesn't have the same negative impact on her.

You feel a glimmer of hope, though. You can see that the severity of this situation is starting to sink in a bit. You are getting somewhere. You press on.

You explain that you are bothered by her apparent lack of desire for you. Nothing you do ever turns her on. You're always turned on by HER, but she can't seem to be able to muster up the energy to reciprocate. *Is it that you just don't love me anymore?"* you ask with tears in your eyes.
She starts crying and explaining.

She's under stress, she says. The house. The kids. Work. It's all just too much to bear at times. All of these things prevent her from getting into the headspace necessary for sexual arousal. She never even thinks about sex. It's not you, it's her. *"Just be patient and understanding with me. Okay?"*
You hold her. You tell her you're sorry. You'll help more around the house. You'll get the kids three days a week after school instead of two. You'll be there more for her, emotionally. You've not been the best partner. You can do better.

She appreciates your help and thanks you for being such a great husband and friend.

You kiss. You hug a while. More crying. She gets up to make dinner. You run off to play with the kids.

Later that night, you go to bed and see her already asleep under the covers. You give her a gentle kiss and go to the basement with your laptop and jerk off to porn. Again. Still, if you're being honest, you DO feel a lot better about your situation. Communication is important, after all. It feels good to get all that off your chest. You finally feel like you may be moving the relationship in the right direction.

Another month will go by. Still no sex with your wife. More rejection. More ignoring you. The heightened sense of energy and hope that you experienced after your big anxiety-fueled talk has quickly dissipated. Your not-so-subtle sexual remarks and hints seem to go completely unnoticed. You left new lingerie sitting out on the bed, and she didn't even see them. They were scooped up and thrown in the wash along with the bed sheets. The wife was pissed that her white sheets are now pink because of the "stupid red lingerie" you bought her.

This is not going as planned.

One night you decide to be less subtle and just go for it. You reach to put your arm around her from behind and she instinctively spins and shoves an elbow into your side, knocking the wind out of you. She apologizes profusely. *"I was just trying to hold you and give you a kiss,"* you explain. *"Why would you do that?!"* she asks.

You decide it's time to have "The Talk" again.

Subsequent conversations with your wife won't be so sweet.

She'll become more frustrated with you. The emotional facade goes away and is replaced with anger and annoyance. She doesn't want to talk about it. *"This is not a big deal,"* she says. *"All of my friends say their marriage is the same. Why can't you just be happy?"*

It feels like you are roommates, or worse… siblings.

More talking. More emotional vomiting. More anger. The cycle continues.

Hammer this into your head, my friend: "The Talk" doesn't work.

"The Talk" just reaffirms what she already knows deep down: You are not the kind of guy she wants to have sex with.

What you are doing is looking for her help. You're asking her to fix the problem. You are putting yourself in a subservient role. You are like a child looking up to mommy to fix his booboo.

This is a gigantic female libido-killer.

Each talk just drives one thing into her brain: *"Oh God. I married a guy who just doesn't GET IT and he probably never will."*

When you pour your guts out to your wife, you're trying to appeal to her rational side:

"Don't you remember how much we love each other? Remember all our good times? Remember all those loving and romantic feelings we used to have for each other? Intimacy is a choice. I love you and choose to want you sexually ALL the time. I don't understand why you refuse to make the same decision."

Instead of appealing to her rational mind, you are setting off an instinctual response that pushes her libido in the wrong direction. Rationality doesn't enter into the world of eroticism and animalistic desire that you want and need so badly. Having "The Talk" with your wife is like walking into the middle of a funeral and performing a strip tease.

If "The Talk" was truly an open and honest conversation, it would go something like this:

You: *"Why don't we have sex more often?"*

Her: *"Because you don't turn me on."*

You: *"Okay, what do I need to do to turn you on more?"*

Her: *"If I have to tell you what to do, then it turns me off even more. I don't even know, to be honest. You should just know what to do. I want a guy who just KNOWS."*

You: *"Well then there's no hope for me, right?"*

Her: *"Probably not. Up to you."*

You: *"So, is that it? We should just divorce?"*

Her: *"Maybe, but that would be ugly and cost us a lot of money and cause the kids irreparable, long-term harm. How about instead we just keep this up for a while until one of us has an affair?"*

You: *"Alright, cool. I'll be in the basement."*

Her: *"Okay. Enjoy jerking off. Loser."*

Everything else said in "The Talk" is just bullshit. "The Talk" is just two people tap-dancing around the bigger picture. Everyone is ignoring the elephant in the room: She just isn't turned on.

"The Talk" is one of the worst things you can do to try and reignite sexual desire.

I understand you have a lot of things on your mind, and you feel sad and want to let your partner know. The problem is that she doesn't like being emotionally dumped on by her man. She certainly doesn't want to be reminded of how she no longer has sexual desire for you. She may actually feel bad about that fact, too. She may feel like a failure of a wife. She may WANT to want you… but her body is saying, "Nope."

For her, the world already feels like it's spinning out of control at times. She wasn't lying about all the pressure she's under. Sometimes it is just too much. You're just adding to the stress of life instead of being the escape she wants and needs so badly.

She doesn't want YOUR problems on top of the giant pile of her OWN problems. Especially when the underlying cause of your problems can be summed up as: *"You know... you're kind of a shitty wife."*

Yes, she complains about everything to you ALL THE FUCKING TIME. Yes, you may feel that you should be able to do the same when it comes to your lack of sex. No, you cannot. Yes, it's a double standard. Yes, it's sexist. Sorry, that's real life. Why do you think for centuries men have bottled up their insecurities and emotions and only have deep talks with select guy friends?

Because nobody else, especially your wife, will give a shit about you not getting the sex you feel you so richly deserve.

"But, that's not what she said."

Your wife may ask you to please open up to her and trust her with your feelings. She may say she doesn't feel close as a couple unless you let her know what's going on with you and why you're so down lately.

She wants you to be vulnerable.

Vulnerability IS a good thing. It can be argued that there's real strength in vulnerability. The problem is that for many of you, your anxieties are such that you don't know when to stop. You emote… and emote… and emote. It's too much. To compound the difficulty of the situation, every woman has a different threshold for when it hits the "too much" point. Some women roll their eyes and talk bad about their spouse because he has a fever of 103 and feels sick as a dog. *"Oh god, he's such a baby."* Other women are there for their husband through thick and thin, see him at his worst, and still remain his biggest cheerleader. If you're reading this book… I'm willing to bet your wife is not the cheerleader type, is she?

First of all, your wife absolutely knows what is going on in your head. You've been begging her for sex in one way or another for quite some time. Again, she knows that men are usually way more horny than women. It's not some well-kept secret. To her, everything you do at home seems to revolve around trying to get in her pants.

So then, why would she ask you to open up if she doesn't want to hear it?

Well, this can be construed as one of those "tests" that we talked about earlier. Almost every married man has experienced something similar to this scenario:

Her: *"Please tell me what is wrong. I'm your wife. You need to share these things with me. I love you. I'm here for you."*

Him: *"Okay… well, [insert massive amounts of emotional vomiting here]."*

Her: *"Well… I'm going to need some time alone to process this. Just… no… don't touch me right now. Just… leave me alone for a while."*

Your wife is not wired to listen to her man endlessly emote. To quote author and psychotherapist Esther Perel:

"Men are afraid of women's tensions, but women are afraid of men's meltdowns—that they will regress, suddenly going from man to boy to baby. Women believe that men are more fragile on some fundamental level, and they think that if they let loose, they'll fall apart. Many women don't trust in the emotional resilience of men. They think they are superior in this realm."

Many women are also afraid that if they soften their partner, then they won't be able lean on him. They fundamentally still want him to be strong, because that allows them to fall apart: 'I need to know that you can hold me and that you're strong. If you're not strong, I can't let go.' This is true in sex, and this is true emotionally. If/when for some reason he softens, there is a part of her that feels angry. Instead of becoming compassionate, she becomes angry."

Your wife is especially not wired to listen to her husband complain about what she already knows deep down inside: She is not sexually aroused within the confines of this relationship.

YOU do not turn HER on.

Instead of endlessly emoting and asking her to fix the problem, you might as well sit her down, start crying, and repeatedly yell in her face, "I'M NOT ATTRACTIVE! I'M NOT ATTRACTIVE! I'M NOT ATTRACTIVE!"

She would LOVE to come home every day to a rock of a man who is strong no matter what is going on in the world. She wants a guy she can collapse into, somebody to make her feel safe and loved.

Instead, she has this whiny little husband who is repeatedly asking her for sex and yapping about his nonsense, like a Chihuahua begging for scraps from the dinner table.

Not good. Not manly. Not attractive. Very needy.

When you talk to your woman about her lack of libido, you might as well be talking to the sky about the lack of rain. You'll get the same result.

Yes, after much whining, your wife may eventually throw you a bone just to shut you up. She'll finally cave in and have the dreaded "pity sex" with you: *"Fine… let's do this. But hurry up, my show is coming on in 10 minutes."*

But, if we're being honest, we don't like it. Not at all. We really don't want a lifeless mannequin lying in bed with her legs open saying, *"Fuck me. Please. You stallion. Take me. Oh god. Yes,"* as she blankly stares off into space, like some sarcastic monotone robot.

We want passion.

We want to be desired.

We want a woman who can't help herself.

We want to feel like a man again.

TALKING and rationalizing with your wife will never bring this about.

You're thinking like a dude: *"I want sex every day. I have a penis. You have a vagina. I'm turned on just thinking about it. Let's do this."*

Remember, you are engineered to do this. You get erect if the wind blows just right. In case you couldn't tell, your wife is not built the same.

To get your wife's engine going within the confines of your long-term, monogamous marriage requires a delicate recipe akin to a soufflé. One wrong move and the whole thing collapses.

You've been making wrong moves for years now. One little chat is not going to resolve this. Hundreds of chats won't result in carnal desire.

We're talking about emotion. Nature. Human nature. Our innate programming. You can't beat that with reason and logic.

Stop trying. Stop talking.

The programming doesn't give a shit.

CHAPTER 3
NICE GUYS
FINISH LAST

"If you're ever yelling at a woman, all you should be saying is, 'Why can't you be my mommy? Why are you NOT my mommy?'"

—Marc Maron

The Five Mistakes All Have One Thing in Common

Their methods and expected outcomes are not grounded in reality. They are all grounded in the world of what SHOULD be. They're all from the typical "Nice Guy" book of rules.

X does not seem to result in Y… but, dammit, it should! This concept of "should" is getting you nowhere in life. You're stomping your feet like a child and screaming, "IT'S NOT FAIR! I'M A REALLY GREAT GUY!! WHERE'S MY SEX?!" How's that working out for you?

You are attempting to apply your logic, reason, and a sense of right and wrong to a world where the most basic and instinctual behavior reigns supreme.

You can't out-nice her lack of sexual desire. The world of sexual desire is governed by instinct. It's controlled by thousands and thousands of years of programming that is deeply embedded into our DNA.

Sometimes, the programming is predictable:

> *"If young pretty woman with nice skin and a sexy shape looks at me, smiles, and plays with her hair ->Then activate erection sequence for quick copulation."*

Sometimes, the programming is confusing:

"If skinny, androgynous heroin-addicted rock star looks at me -> Then pump blood to vulva to increase chances of successful intercourse and fertilization."

But, there's absolutely nothing in that programming that says:

"If sweet, well-intentioned male that promised to love me unconditionally forever whines incessantly and begs me for sex -> Then activate immediate fornication sequence."

This programming is not nice. It is not politically correct. It does not care about you and your feelings. It doesn't take into consideration the last 100 years of progressive societal change. In evolutionary terms, that's a fraction of a blink of an eye.

The programming certainly doesn't care about your past ten years of being a great dad and loving partner. The programming laughs at your Nice Guy behavior.

Yes, the programming is a major asshole.

And yet, we all think we can outsmart this programming, don't we? I certainly don't blame you for trying. We seem to control everything else around us, so why not human sexuality? Surely, we can rise above the shallowness of caveman programming and become deeper, more thoughtful human beings and set aside all this shallow bullshit, right?

Unfortunately, no. We keep trying to rewrite the programming… and we keep failing. We may have temporary success (awful pity sex), but the end result is the same: The wife is just even more turned off than before. The passion you so desire is still out of reach. It remains a distant memory.

Been there, done that, along with millions of other men.

The Five Mistakes are rooted in the belief that the sexual machine we have in us is inherently moral and rooted in rationality. We think that our status as the planet's most intelligent creature allows us to easily overcome our animalistic programming. We think we live day-to-day in a world that we can manipulate via our free will. We extend that mindset to matters where it's laughably wrong.

We think our wife has a choice of whether to be sexually aroused.

She doesn't.

Yes, she can physically walk to the bedroom, take off her clothes, open her legs, and say, *"Go ahead. Get it over with."* What she can't do is flip the switch that turns on TRUE sexual desire.

Going through the motions does not mean she is aroused. It just means she's trying to shut you up and get it over with so she can move on to more important things.

You don't want that. None of us want that.

It's time to throw in the towel and listen to the primal machine for once. It's not going anywhere. It's been there for thousands of generations.

You Can't "Nice" Your Way into Her Pants

To illustrate, I don't care what kind of flirtatious skills or awesome personality she may have, I cannot get aroused by a 900-pound woman with a beard. She can tell me what a dirty slut she is, and how she won the "Best Blowjobs in Texas" award 10 years in a row… but she can't overcome my innate programming that screams, "RUN FOR YOUR LIFE!!"

Same rule applies to your situation.

"Dude… are you calling me a 900-pound bearded woman?"

Yes. Yes, I am.

I don't care how many bags of trash you take out, how many purses you buy her, what kind of fancy SUV you lease for her, how many long and deep conversations about your awful sex life you may have… These things just can't get her sexual engine going.

In fact, they may put you farther down the shitty hole you are trying to escape from. Why? Because you just don't get it. Her programming wants somebody who GETS it; her programming is looking for a match to its primal needs. The more you keep committing the same mistakes, the more you just reinforce the negative instinctual response she has lingering deep in her programming.

No wonder you're in a dead bedroom.

Let's be honest… your wife loves you. She appreciates all you do for her and the kids. She values your friendship and partnership over the years. She may indeed consider you the love of her life. She may plan to live with you until the day she dies.

None of that can overcome the hindbrain sending her repeated signals that say: "ABORT SEXUAL RESPONSE. THIS MALE IS NOT FIT FOR REPRODUCTION." Those signals may not be strong enough for her to divorce you, but those signals are what keep her comfy sweatpants on night after night. She may have very well resigned herself to the fact that this is "normal" for marriage. She may have very well grown up seeing this dynamic at home with her parents (more on this later).

Nothing can reverse that programming… except somebody who truly does turn her on.

You simply want her to look at you, bite her lip, take her clothes off, and drag you into the bedroom?

That is a primal reaction. This requires primal action on your part.

You can't drag desire out of her with kindness and understanding.

It sucks… but it's true.

Nice guys do, in fact, finish last.

Stop Putting the Poor Woman on a Pedestal

Look, I get it. You're a good man. You have a good heart. You love your wife, and you just want that passion back again. You're having a hard time balancing your basic horny male programming with your rational brain telling you that you love your wife and she's your best friend, partner, and mom to your kids.

This doesn't change the fact that she's every bit as flawed as you are. You have worshiped this poor woman for far too long.

Your wife farts. She takes dumps. She gets pimples. She has wrinkles. She has cellulite. She smells bad if she doesn't shower. She's also completely devoid of superpowers. In fact, she is probably physically weaker than you are.

She's a human being.

I know… you've been told to always be a gentleman. Treat her like a queen. "Happy wife, happy life." She's the fairer sex, after all, a delicate flower that requires great care. You need to keep your stew of toxic masculinity on a low simmer or else you'll risk being an abusive asshole and scare her away.

This "soft" theme permeates your actions as well as your results.

Your gifts, your chore play, your lying, your tiptoeing, your constant talking and seeking reassurance… they all have the theme of *"Please, Your Highness, am I now worthy of your affection?"*

It's all a variation on one theme: neediness. It's also a manifestation of your anxiety. A needy, anxious man is not attractive by any measure.

Every time you try one of the Five Mistakes, you are striking the proverbial chisel. Piece by piece, you are building a marble effigy in your wife's image. The placard on the front reads, *"My wife. She's now a giant bitch that never wants sex with me. I still worship her, though. I need her. Without her, I am lost."*

Contrary to popular belief, she doesn't want to be the ruler of your world. She doesn't want you to worship her. She doesn't want you to NEED her. She wants YOU to be the marble statue, not her. She wants to be able to point across the crowded room and say to her friends, *"That's MY MAN right there!"*

How can she look up to you and respect you if she's looking down on you?

If she doesn't respect you, she's not fucking you.

"My wife told me that she loves my good-natured sweet side. She told me she wanted to see more of that. She likes it when I cater to her. She hates it when I act any other way. She says

that turns her off and ruins any chance we have for future sex."

Listen to her… smile… and observe.

What she DOES is far more important than what she SAYS. Or, in your case, what she's NOT doing (having sex with you) is more important than what she says. You're listening to a woman who is not attracted to you tell you that the key to her attraction is to "keep being you" or "amplify your traits even further."

That makes zero sense.

Do you want me to share the countless stories from men who started snooping on their cold, sexless wives and found dirty diaries and photos of them doing crazy, now forbidden sexual acts with ex-boyfriends? She was able to get to that elusive erotic headspace with "losers" from her past, but she just can't bring herself to do the same with her loving and devoted husband of twenty years: *"I was a different girl back then. I've changed!"*

Do you want to hear about the guy who could never get his wife to do oral sex with him because she said that it was "gross" and "that sort of thing is for porn," only to find a video of her having a threesome last week with a guy and another woman from her Crossfit class?

How about the countless sexually frustrated men who stare angrily at their wives' well-worn vibrators and growing stack of filthy romance novels?

Your wife has sexual/intimacy needs, too. She's a human being. Right now, those needs are either dormant and waiting to come out for the right guy—smothered by the domesticity of your long-term relationship—or they are already out and she is screwing around behind your back.

"But, she said…"

She will SAY whatever she feels you want to hear. Your actions over the years have probably told her that you are a pretty sensitive guy. Your anxiety is very obvious to her and everyone around you. She doesn't want to see a pouty, whining man sulking around the house… so she keeps her true feelings to herself.

You can think of this as her version of "happy wife, happy life." An anxious, whiny, and beaten man makes her also feel very anxious and sometimes very angry. She would prefer not to go to that emotional space, if possible. Saying, *"It's not you, it's me,"* or *"Just be you,"* keeps your anxieties at bay.

If you are wealthy Mr. Provider Extraordinaire, or Best Dad in the Universe, then she REALLY doesn't want to rock the relationship boat. She has a good thing going. "It's not you, it's me" buys her more time. Maybe she'll throw you some pity sex to keep you quiet for a while. She must keep the Provider's resource machine humming along.

On the other hand, she truly may NOT know why she has

no desire for you anymore. All she knows is that the switch got turned off some time ago and nothing seems to be able to turn it back on. Sex just isn't on her mind anymore.

"Maybe I'm just asexual," she says, or worse, *"Maybe I'm a broken person."*

A surprisingly large number of women are completely clueless about what gets their sexual engine going. Ironically, they too feel like they SHOULD be aroused and ready to have sex with their husband… but man, they just can't muster the energy and bring about the mindset necessary to get to that level of intimacy and eroticism with their loving spouse. Faking it and pity sex kills them inside just as much as it does the husband.

Many women will openly talk with their friends about sex. They will report back to the husband (after enduring one of his many talks): *"A lot of women are like me. We just don't want sex that much after we have kids. It's natural. There's nothing wrong with that."*

Yes, it is perfectly natural and predictable behavior. That is until somebody else comes along and gets their sexual engine going again. That sexual reawakening is just as natural and just as predictable.

My experience shows that when these "low libido" women DO wake up from their sexual slumber (usually in the form of a new relationship)… oh boy, watch out. "Sexual deviance" doesn't begin to cover it. "Slut" is not a strong enough word. These women rediscover a part of themselves that they completely forgot ever existed. The sexual bomb that goes off is something amazing to behold. Ask any guy who watches his ex-wife post-divorce lose fifty pounds and seem to become twenty years younger. Her new sexual persona is perplexing and angering.

"Where was that energy when she was with me?!"

Many guys who discover their wives are having an affair will witness the same thing. The same behavioral mechanism is at play.

"This isn't my wife," these men will say. *"She's acting crazy."*

No, it's your wife. It's always been your wife. She's not "crazy," she's in love. She's turned on; she's back on the market again. People in love sometimes do wacky, irrational stuff. They make some major life mistakes. They move across the country. They quit their jobs. They act foolish and irresponsible. They are like crazy and rebellious teenagers. They also have lots of sex. They are drunk on lust. They are addicts. You were probably that way too, once.

I know lots of men who have done some CRAZY things for a girl.

You want to generate this type of "crazy" response in your wife. She wants that, too.

Big Picture Question: Do You, Mr. Nice Guy, REALLY Want Sex from Your Wife?

Two big questions you need to ask yourself:

1. Do you REALLY want your wife?
2. Are you REALLY willing to make the changes needed to improve your sex life?

Let's first break down question number one. Here's a common scenario I hear from men I chat with during one-on-one sessions (you can book your own session with me at helpformen.com):

Reader: *"Man my wife is just awful. She does all of these horrible things on a regular basis. She treats me poorly. She talks down to me. She hasn't touched me in ten years. She's gained 100 pounds. She sometimes goes without bathing. She makes zero attempt at making herself look good. I actually caught her texting other men several times. She refuses to talk to me about our issues. She acts like everything is fine."*

Me: *"Okay, yeah… that's all pretty awful. So, what is your goal here with this relationship?"*

Reader: *"Well, I read The Dead Bedroom Fix, so obviously I want more sex from my wife."*

Let's stop and think about this. The man just told me, in grueling detail, about just what an awful human being his wife is. His next thought: *"So... where's my sex?"*

The kicker in these scenarios is that the wife KNOWS she is not a good wife. She KNOWS she is treating her husband poorly. She KNOWS that she has been building a case for winning the "Worst Wife Ever" prize year after year. And yet... here comes Mr. Erection again: *"So... wanna have sex?"*

What does that mean to the wife? *"He doesn't actually want ME, he just wants sexual gratification."* Basically, you want to use your wife as a big, angry masturbation device. In her mind, there's no attempt at real connection. There's no real effort to become somebody who she actually wants. There's no longer any attempt at playing the mating game in any way... beyond just pressuring her so that you can use her as a warm hole.

You don't want her as a person. No sane man would. She's an objectively awful partner in every way. Yet... you want her, sexually. That's not good, my man.

Does your wife fit into this scenario? Do you, in fact, just want to use her to fulfill your needs, rather than want her because of your genuine lust and desire for HER as a person? When she walks across the room, do you find your eyes following her and saying to yourself, *"God, she is so gorgeous"*? When she does something for you and the family, do you look at her and say, *"She is one amazing wife. I just love her to death*"? Do you have genuine love, admiration, appreciation, and lust for your wife?

It surprises me how many men hesitate at this line of questioning. What should be a knee-jerk response of, "Yes, of course! I'm crazy about her!" is instead one of quiet realization: "*Wow… I guess I really don't like my wife. Never thought about it like that.*"

If this is your case, you have a lot of work to do. You have a lot of introspection and deep thinking to do about you, your relationship, and your future as either her husband or as a newly single man.

Now, on to question number two: **Are you REALLY willing to make the changes needed to improve your sex life?**

Let's assume that you still have genuine love, admiration, appreciation, and lust for your wife. Don't think for a minute that things will be much easier for you. The question I have posed may seem silly (after all, you bought this book, right?), but we're talking about altering your reality here. We're talking about doing stuff that is most likely WAY outside of your comfort zone. I can't stress enough how, for many of you, this will be a complete 180 from how you have done things up to this point in your marriage.

If you're reading this book, you are probably an anxious guy. As an anxious guy, you do NOT like doing things outside of your comfort zone. After all, many of you are enduring a relationship that a low-anxiety guy would've probably pulled the plug on years ago. Instead, your anxiety and codependency keep you attached in a very unhealthy way. For some jackass like me to come along and completely flip your world upside down may be very upsetting.

In other words, this isn't going to be easy for you. Not by a long shot.

Some guys get into this transformational process and say, *"Alright… you know what? Nope. Not happening. I'm going back to the old me."* Years later they are still where they were before, or worse. I talk to these guys ALL the time.

You gotta have balls to make real change. You need courage. You need the willingness to fail again and again. You must set aside your "fragile male ego." You can't tiptoe your way out of this mess. You need to put your helmet on and run head-first into the brick wall.

Think of a skill that you have practiced for years, something you consider yourself to be pretty good at. For me, it would be coaching and running this Dad Starting Over and Help For Men business.

As far as my little world of clients and fans is concerned, I'm pretty good at what I do. A lot of people look up to me and lean on me for advice.

As far as the rest of the world is concerned, I'm just average. I'm not that big a deal. I have about 150,000 people following me on YouTube, 150,000 on Facebook, and

130,000 on TikTok… not bad. But there are guys out there who would laugh at those numbers. They have MILLIONS of subscribers and followers. They make six-figure incomes PER MONTH. Wow. Maybe I should just hang it up now and go get a real "job."

Or, I can learn from those guys and keep plowing ahead and continue to reach more people with my material. I will make mistakes as I go, lose money, make money, and help a lot of men on the journey.

The process of learning never stops.

That's not a bad thing. Learning is good. Sometimes it means setting aside my preconceived notions of how to do something. I just need to shut up, listen and learn.

Mentors are amazing; they are worth their weight in gold. They can save you from making tons of mistakes and they allow you to get results you wouldn't otherwise obtain… and get them much faster. To expedite the process of being successful, you need to work with and learn from others. That's all there is to it.

(Speaking of mentors, check out our team of coaches at helpformen.com/coaching)

So, with the mentoring philosophy in mind, is there anybody else in your little world who would be a great mentor for how to cultivate a sexy relationship with women? No? Can't think of a single person? Are you sure about that?

Think back on your life from puberty up until today. Remember your teen years. Who got all of the girls? Who was Mr. Popular? Which kid in school got laid first? How about in college? Who was just swimming in coeds and had to beat them off with a stick? Who would always sneak girls over to their dorm room? Who has the happy, sexy MILF of a wife that all the other dads drool over?

Got the image of the guy in mind? What do all these guys have in common? What do they DO? To get your wife's engine going again, you will need to emulate some basic behaviors that you have, ironically, observed your whole life. That's right, for YEARS you were given up-close lessons on how to score sex, but you ignored them, or at the very least downplayed their importance.

Those same lessons apply now to your marriage.
The steps you must take to generate desire are steps that you have continuously dismissed as shallow, stupid, manipulative, and archaic. You have convinced yourself that you are above the silly mating game:

- "I don't play games."
- "Ha! I don't have to do that stuff… I'm married."

Oh yeah? No games? You're above that bullshit? Ok, cool.

How's that working out for you?

Exactly.

Set aside your prejudices. Ignore your advanced college degree. Forget what mom told you.

Pretend you don't have a cultured, more enlightened, and morally superior outlook on life, love, and marriage… and just listen. Watch and learn. You don't have to listen to me. You can follow the endless examples you see around you every single day.

I'll be honest with you; I'm a real softy. I'm a sensitive dude. I'm your quintessential "sweet" guy. I love babies, cute animals, playing with my kids, art, music, romance… and I always have. That's me. I'm not talking about changing who you are. I'm talking about stepping out of your comfort zone and recognizing that sometimes you must do things in a completely different manner to get the result you want. Sometimes that means setting aside what you think is "good" and "kind." Very often, it's just you hiding behind your anxieties. It's you flexing your people-pleaser muscle. Believe it or not, it's often just you being manipulative and needy.

We're going back to high school-level stuff here. We're going over the stuff that Dad or your older brother should've taught you but didn't. Maybe they did try, but their advice was drowned out by well-intentioned girls and friends telling you to "just be yourself."

Sound like I'm talking about dating or how to pick up girls?

Yeah… we are, in a sense. What, you thought all that ended when you got married? You thought you would "outgrow" all that silly BS?

Not even close, cowboy.

You need that silly BS now more than ever.

It's okay, we've all been there. Some of us learn the lesson the hard way. Some of us never get that chance and we die after having decades of a mediocre and unfulfilling sex life and marriage. Some of us learn that our wife was a super sexual person… but only with other men. Some of us learn that our wife fell out of love with us years ago and only hung around for the safety and security that we provide.

NOT you, though. You're going to say, *"To hell with all that."*

You're going to turn this around.

CHAPTER 4
BE HER LOVER

"A successful marriage requires falling in love many times, always with the same person."

—Mignon McLaughlin

I Don't Have to Do That Shit Anymore. I'm Married

Years ago, shortly after my divorce, I was at my oldest boy's wrestling practice and chatting with another dad. We were roughly the same age. He said he noticed me lifting weights the other day at the gym we both attended. He told me he was just doing cardio at the time to lose weight, but he was impressed with my weightlifting.

Then he did what all out-of-shape older guys do: He started bragging about how he USED to be Awesome Mr. Weightlifter Guy back in the day.

Him: *"I could bench 315 for 10 reps when I was in college."* *Wow. Never heard that one before.*

I indulged him a little. I told him that he was stronger than I'd ever been. I told him that I now skip the bench press and use dumbbells instead because of my shoulder pain, how I need to stretch way more, it takes me longer to recuperate… He cut me off. He didn't want to hear it.

Him: *"Yeah, well… I don't have to do any of that shit anymore. I'm married."*

See, he knew at the time that I was divorced and dating. My wife leaving me was a big event in our small circle of wrestling parents.

Here's the subtext of what he was really saying:

"You have to do all that building and maintaining your body because you are looking for a new woman. I already have one. No need to keep up the charade."

There's an understood dynamic at play in the post-divorce/single dating world. We instinctively recognize our need to lower our "Provider" traits and amplify our "Lover" traits. We hit the gym, dress nicer, get more frequent haircuts, get a sportier car, etc.

All of this gives the appearance of being "fun" and "good-looking." We want to appear more youthful and energetic. We know that if we want the girl of our dreams, we must look and play the part of the "Lover." After all, we're in hunting mode. We instinctively know the best way to attract our prey.

Both men and women play this mating game. The ex-wife gets the tattoo, the nose piercing, loses forty pounds, and suddenly dresses in a much more youthful way. She may say that she suddenly feels free to devote time to herself (and she's right), but what she may fail to realize is that there is also a very instinctual mating dance at play here. She innately knows what it takes to attract a new mate, just like her ex-husband who now pays $30 a month to join the gym that he used to drive by every day on the way to work for the past fifteen years.

We instinctively know what to do when playing the mating

game. You amplify the "shallow" stuff. You don't approach a pretty little thing at the bar and say, *"Hey there. I'm Ralph. I'm really good at ironing and folding laundry."*

Later, when we finally land a woman and marry her, the universal understanding is that you must now flip the scales in favor of Provider mode. You can let the stupid Lover stuff go… it's no longer needed. We, as men, must then focus on being a Provider above all else. We drop the sexy hobbies, pick up the beer bottle and the Oreos, and lose all semblance of sexual attraction.

It's our own form of the classic "bait and switch."

This is the wrong thing to do on so many levels.

You want to be your wife's Lover. Always. If you're not, then somebody or something else will eventually give her that emotional and physical high that she needs.

Saying "I do" shouldn't change your mating habits. In fact, ironically, it means that you must ramp up your Lover qualities even more. Why? Because now that she has a committed husband, your wife will also naturally start to get more comfortable. In the world of the woman's libido, comfort does not correspond to sexual desire. I repeat, COMFORT DOES NOT CORRESPOND TO SEXUAL DESIRE.

To quote psychotherapist Esther Perel:

"The intense physical and emotional fusion [new lover's] experience is possible only with someone we don't yet know. At this early stage merging and surrendering are relatively safe, because the boundaries between the two people are still externally defined. [The lovers] are new to each other. And while they are migrating into each other's respective worlds, they have not yet taken full residence; they are still two distinct entities. It is all the space between them that allows them to imagine no space at all…

In the beginning, you can focus on the connection because the psychological distance is already there; it's a part of the structure. Otherness is a fact. You don't need to cultivate separateness in the early stages of falling in love; you still are separate."

In other words, you aim for comfort, intimacy, and prolonged connectivity… but that is precisely what kills the passion we feel in the early stages of the relationship.
But, wait… comfort is what you want to provide, right? You want to help put a roof over her head. Food on the table. Be there for her when things go wrong. Help her when she is sick, right?

Yes, of course. Keep doing those things. They're wonderful things. That's part of being an awesome human being. This is the essence of being a good life partner.

But realize that these things don't result in a horny wife and a wild sex life. You can't just put all your eggs in the Provider basket and hope for a porn star level of activity in the bedroom.

A romantic relationship that is built solely on Provider points is not sustainable.

The Marriage Landscape Has Drastically Changed

Guys, some of you are playing by a very old and outdated book of marriage rules. I'm sorry to have to break this to you, but the 1950s are over. These days, in many parts of the world, full-time housewives are a very rare thing. In fact, women overall are now more educated than ever. Women make up the majority of our university student population and more women than men graduate with a degree. Women are more career-focused. They excel at their jobs and reach high-performance levels and rank within their companies. Suzy Homemaker is not completely dead, but she's on life support.

Does this new role in life make women happier and more fulfilled human beings? No, of course not. They are as unhappy as ever. (Welcome to the pointless rat race, ladies.) What it does do is give them more options in life. Having more freedom reinforces the concept of *"I really don't have to live like this if I don't want to."*

We know ladies are fickle by nature. One day she loves something… the next day she hates it with a burning passion and has a completely rational (and lengthy) explanation as to why she had a sudden change of heart. Now, apply this same fickle mindset to marriage.

Women initiate 70% of divorces. We know that the higher the woman's income is, the more likely she is to divorce.

If she makes more money than her husband, she is more likely to divorce. If the husband is a stay-at-home father, the chances of divorce go up 32% (if you are to believe the controversial Harvard study).

It seems that there are quite a few conditions that can lead to marital dissatisfaction for women. If they're not happy, they're leaving and taking their BMW with them.

For most of us, long gone are the days of the man coming home from a long day at work, taking off his hat, and expecting a stiff drink and a hot meal waiting for him. There's no innate reward for being the breadwinner with the penis. The man must find other ways to earn the title of "good husband." The paycheck and pointless job title just don't cut it anymore. She already has or can have those things, too. In fact, for many of you reading this, your wife makes more money than you… or has the potential to do so. She's one promotion away from leaving you in the dust.

What if you do happen to make more money than her? Unfortunately, as many of my readers have learned, there are these little things called "divorce," "alimony," and "child support" that can very quickly take care of that. Millions of men have discovered this awesome trifecta of soul-crushing, state-mandated resource allocation.

The wife doesn't have to endure a boring and unfulfilling marriage anymore. All the barriers between her and a more fulfilling life have been eliminated. She's a free woman. Want to be in a happy and sexual relationship with one woman for the rest of your life? You got your work cut out for you, amigo.

Another thing that has changed in a big way is that women are now having affairs more than ever.

Many men who reach out to me for coaching have experienced the pain of discovering their wife's affair. A big percentage of those affairs were precipitated by some type of life-altering event that served as the relationship's tipping point. Sometimes it was stressful and terrible (like death or illness), but many times the straw that broke the marriage camel's back was something simple like the wife landing a big promotion at work or just having a little extra money in her paycheck.

It's really very simple: At some point in the relationship, she naturally loses sexual interest in her husband. Comfort, familiarity, and boredom set in, but she stays with him for the security and resources that the marriage provides. Then, through her own hard work, she achieves the ability to make her own money. She then has an epiphany: There is no longer a "need" for her husband.

"He's not fun… He doesn't turn me on… I don't really like him all that much anymore… I make more money than he does… So, what am I doing with him again?"

That's when she throws aside her boundaries that were so necessary for maintaining fidelity. Her "must find new mate" programming is activated. Ironically, she usually runs off and has an affair with a man who, by pretty much everyone's standards, is a complete and total loser.

Everyone: *"I don't get it... Him?!"*

Sure, her affair partner may not be gainfully employed, may live in his parents' basement, may drive a shitty car, and may have a criminal record... but he's fun, interesting, and something about him pushes her buttons. He makes her feel sexy again. He taps into something that makes her "feel alive." He allows her to temporarily strip herself of the boring veneer of "wife" and "mom."

In her mind, she is rediscovering her "real" self.

The societal pressure is miraculously lifted from her shoulders, one orgasm at a time.

He's her Lover. He is no Provider. She knows that. That's precisely what she likes about him.

Next thing you know, she is wiping the marriage scoreboard clean. All those Provider points you have earned over the years mean exactly zero when somebody comes along and pushes those oft-neglected *"I-am-an-independent-sexual-creature"* buttons of hers.

Men who are left by their wives start listing all the wonderful things they did as Provider for her and the family. He's building the case for why her affair is completely irrational.

Nothing seems to get through to the wife. It's as if she is taken over by a spell. Many people refer to this stage as the "affair fog." She can't see clearly. The vapor of lustfulness surrounds her, obscuring her vision. She can't see the family and loving husband she is destroying. She is only concerned with her feelings.

Mother Nature has taken over; the mating dance has begun. By this point in the relationship, the wife has very real disdain for her husband. Not only is he of no use to her anymore, but he also kept her from feeling "so alive" all those years. He wasn't the all-around perfect man she deserved. He was just an obstacle in the way of true happiness and fulfillment. In her mind, this is unforgivable. The husband is perplexed. This makes no sense—but it's simple, though.

The Lover wins. Every. Single. Time.

So, to be a good husband, you will want to be a good mix of Lover and Provider.

That's what being a "real man" is all about. In fact, I will take it a step further and say your scales should be tipped more to the Lover side when in a marriage. You want a good helping of the fun, flirty, kinda dangerous, charming, ambitious, sexy tough guy that could bang a pretty woman this week if he wanted to… with a good healthy serving of sweet Provider guy thrown in there.

If you're like most guys I chat with, you probably have the

Provider role down pat. You can do all those great family-oriented things in your sleep. You've probably heard: *"You're such a good/nice guy,"* more than a few times in your life. Because of your childhood baggage, you may even have real shame and disgust tied to the more "manly" and "masculine" Lover side of you. You may have an untapped wealth of skills and natural abilities that you aren't even aware of.

It's time to dive into your Lover side and turn that knob up to eleven. It's been stuck at zero for far too long.

You may surprise yourself with the results.

Be Her Lover Step #1: Go to the Gym

The Lover, more often than not, is a good-looking and low-anxiety dude. Not always, of course, but usually. Contrary to popular belief, "good looks" is not a subjective thing. People know "handsome" and "beautiful" when they see it.

Similarly, we also know ugly when we see it.

Science can break down what makes a man "attractive" to women across all cultures, and the "attractive" traits always point to two things:

1. **Health:** nice teeth, clear skin, high energy, positive attitude

2. **High levels of testosterone:** good musculature, good posture, confidence, aggression, low anxiety

Look good. Look healthy. Be active. Be masculine. Be calm. Be confident. That about covers it. Not so hard, right? Well, some things can very easily get in the way of attaining your "be attractive" goals as a man.

Comfort is thy enemy.

When men enter a long-term, monogamous relationship, it's like a warm and intoxicating bath after a hard day's work. You just settle in, relax, and get comfortable. "Aaaaaah."

No more dating. No more rejection. No more stupid games. No more of all that annoying single-life bullshit. Now you can live a "normal" life. Finally.

But, of course, there's a trade-off. With the comfort of a steady and secure relationship comes a slew of negative repercussions. The first and most obvious is the breakdown of your physical appearance. To put it bluntly, once they say, "I do," both men and women tend to stop focusing on their looks. We gain weight. We stop doing things that build and maintain muscle. Our focus is elsewhere. That shallow physical stuff, as many women report, is just "silly." Instead, we must focus on paying the bills, feeding the kids, and taking part in all the extracurricular activities.

"I would totally go to the gym, but who has the time for that?"

The reality is that it is VERY easy to skip the hard stuff that you really don't HAVE to do. Read more books? Go to the gym? Eat right? Those are tough habits to keep up. They take time... and spare time is something that people today have very little of, right?

Bullshit.

Sorry, I'm not buying it. You're just being lazy.

I have four kids and I work full-time. More than full-time. I also travel back and forth often between two states. My wife works full-time as a medical doctor. I manage to go to the gym five days a week. I also do cardio every single day. I don't eat like shit. My wife had two serious back surgeries that left her incapacitated for a month. As soon as her required bed rest period was over, she was back with a trainer working on regaining her strength and health. She still views working on her body as a habit. There's no question that she has to do it. She's a doctor, she knows how quickly the body can go south if you don't take care of it. Are you too busy taking kids all over the place? Soccer, basketball, football, Boy Scouts, etc.?

Here's a novel idea: Stop trying to impress everyone with how many clubs and sports your kids attend. It's okay if they don't do every activity under the sun. Yes, they can be at home learning how to entertain themselves. They can play with kids in the neighborhood. (There's a novel idea.) If they must attend that underwater fencing class that is so damn important, arrange for them to go with friends every now and then. It's okay for you not to tag along for every single event—that doesn't make you a horrible parent.

Take care of yourself for once. There's nothing wrong with trying to be a better and more healthy man. Ironically, missing one of your kid's seven sports events will, in the long run, make you a better and healthier father to your children.

Let's be honest, getting in shape is not that hard. We're not talking about building a new addition to the house or figuring out how to launch a rocket into space.
We're talking about exercise and eating right. We're talking about personal discipline.

I would just love to eat pizza, drink bourbon, and watch football all day... but I can't. I have three kids to feed. Bills to pay. I have a body to maintain. My fitness is right up there with brushing my teeth and taking showers. It's just something I do; it's a habit.

Bad habits can get in the way of good ones. Eliminate them. Today. You know what they are. Watching stupid, brain-dead television shows, porn, over-eating... we all know they're not good for us. Be honest with yourself. Be a man and cut them out of your life.

Working out is not hugely time-consuming. It's one hour a day, one stupid, little hour.

That one hour can transform you into a MUCH healthier and more energetic man. You will add GOOD years to your life. If that's not reason enough... you will LOOK a lot better, and subsequently:

- Your wife will be more attracted to you.

- Other women will be more attracted to you.

- Your wife will notice the other women being more attracted to you and she will become even MORE attracted to you (don't laugh... it's true).

- You will be less stressed and will have more positive energy. This will result in less emoting to your wife.
- Men will respect you more.

• Your wife will notice men respecting you more and she will become EVEN MORE attracted to you.

• Your chances of getting sex from your wife will go up exponentially. Seriously.

"You don't know my wife, dude. Getting abs won't change anything."

Really? Have you tried? I didn't think so.

"But I shouldn't HAVE to go to the gym! She should just want ME for ME!"

For some men, just the thought of having to get fit to become more attractive is insulting. His wife doesn't look that great, after all, and HE still wants HER! Why can't she just suck it up and do the same?

If you find yourself saying this, you have some serious issues you need to work out. You have issues with your perception of reality. You are, again, the stomping spoiled brat who doesn't get his way. Stop thinking about how things SHOULD be. In fact, completely eliminate the concept of SHOULD from your vocabulary. Seriously. It's done nothing but amplify your victim mentality and it makes you unattractive to everyone around you.

Hey, I'm sorry if somebody sold you on the romantic notion of your wife being sexually aroused by WHO you are and not WHAT you are, but it's simply not the complete truth.

Yes, your wife loves you for YOU, but as I will say again and again in this book to the point of annoyance… your good-natured ways and track record of awesome dad behavior don't push her "must-have-sex" buttons.

What does help push her buttons are a flat stomach, strong pecs, a nice butt, and powerful arms

"But my wife says she's not into muscles. She likes nerdy, sweet guys."

In this book, we are going to keep coming back to the whole concept of *"My wife says…"*

Don't listen to her. Watch her actions instead.

What comes out of her mouth is what she believes you and society want her to say. In her mind, saying she likes a powerful and masculine man will both hurt your feelings (because… well… look at you) and it will also paint her as some kind of shallow, basic simpleton:

"Wait… you like MUSCLES on a guy? What kind of dumb slut are you?"

If she says she's into nerdy, sweet, nice guys, well then society will praise her:

"Oh, you have a deeper and more developed sense of what is truly attractive in men! Good job, thoughtful lady!"

Trust me, women like masculinity, confidence, and power. Think Fifty Shades of Grey. Think every romance novel ever made. You know, those books that are on your wife's Kindle reader… which is conveniently located next to the vibrator in her bedside table.

What says masculinity, confidence, and power more overtly than a strong physique? Note that I'm not talking about the over-the-top steroid-induced bodybuilder physique. Most people find that to look odd, if not comical. No, we're talking about a man's body that looks healthy. A man who looks like he can take care of himself and his wife. A man who can throw his wife over his shoulder and carry her out of a burning building. A man who can roll up his sleeves and chop wood for hours on end.

Since I got into way better shape (thank you testosterone therapy and the gym) I can tell you that looking better is an instant button-pusher for many women, regardless of their age or background. The muscles give the ladies an excuse to act a little more open and sexual than they normally would. They feel safer doing so. Their preoccupation with what their social circle thinks goes right out the window. It's as if all ladies just inherently understand the situation. It's like they all passed out a memo to each other that read:

"Control yourself and your sexuality. Don't act slutty. That's not a good thing. Unless, of course, you're presented with some hunky bombshell of a man. Then you can act like a total moron."

Ever seen footage of a group of women at a bachelorette party with a male stripper? It's insanity. Once the women in the party realize it's okay to act overtly sexual, all bets are off. It can be nothing short of total debauchery. Ironically, it's the complete opposite of a male strip club where all the guys sit like statues and sip their drinks while staring at the naked women. The men don't want to be seen as some kind of creepy perv and thrown out of the place.

The women at the bachelorette party, on the other hand:

"Yes! I get to be a creepy perv! This is fun!"

Oh, the wonderful and confusing animal that is the human being.

For a myriad of reasons, women will often bottle up their very natural and normal human sexuality. They can be a sexual volcano just waiting to blow (pun intended). They just need a good reason to do so and the comfort of knowing they won't be judged for it.

Have you ever had a woman coworker come up to you and squeeze your arm and say, "Nice, Hercules!" or a lady say, "Somebody works out," as she touches your chest? How about a woman lifting your shirt tail to check out your butt? They're not necessarily saying, "I would leave this room and bang you right now," but they are saying:

"Congrats. You pushed a button. You made me do something a little silly and risky. Thanks for that, Mr.

Muscles. That was fun."

All of the above happened to me right away after I lost body fat and gained a good amount of muscle.

"But, dude… my wife HATES muscular athlete type of guys. She says they all look so stupid."

Don't listen to the woman who keeps denying you sex. That's like asking a deer how best to hunt it down and kill it: *"Oh no… keep doing what you're doing! Use that slingshot and that little rock. That's the best way to take me down, by far. Now if you'll excuse me, I'm going to run away very fast in a zigzag pattern so you can't possibly hit me. Good luck!"* Instead, ask the successful hunter with fifty deer heads on his wall: *"You get a 12-gauge shotgun and you shoot them from close range."*

Find a guy who gets lots of sex from his attractive woman (or multiple women) and get his advice. I'll save you some time. You know what they say first and foremost? *"Hit the gym."* They know the mating game is shallow and stupid. They know how much their life changed for the better when they could finally fill out a T-shirt (in a good way).

The guys at the gym get way more tail than you do. Trust me.

Look at it this way: Your body was not meant to be sedentary; it was not meant to sit at a desk all day. The human body has evolved over thousands of years to

MOVE. It was designed to push and pull heavy things, repeatedly. We evolved to walk long distances, climb, lift, and kill creatures that we would then drag back to our tribe to eat. We didn't sit, repeatedly snack, and get fatter and fatter for thousands of years. If we did that, we would have died.

If the majority of women find a fit and healthy-looking man to be more attractive than an overweight and unhealthy man, perhaps this is Mother Nature's way of prompting you to get your butt into shape. In other words, if you want to pass on your genes (via sexual activity with women), you better get your butt moving.

I recognize that there is some pressure among your peers to be a fat lazy slob like they are. I see that every day. I'm almost fifty years of age and I'm one of the oldest guys in my gym. I would say that most guys who work out at my gym on a regular basis are in their twenties.

Most men my age use golf as their main form of exercise. Most of them look like golf balls themselves: round, white, and covered in dimples.

I remember years ago when I asked some fellow dads if they wanted to get together to play basketball at the open gym in town. NOPE. No time. They have kid stuff to do. Work is too busy. Blah blah blah.

Meanwhile, they are playing fantasy football, golfing, watching sports on TV, eating snacks, drinking beer, and, of course, complaining about their pitiful sex lives.

Sad.

They'd rather shove unhealthy food in their faces while watching other men do athletic things. What they don't see is their wife sitting behind them lusting after those football players on TV. She thinks they look really good in their tight pants.

I ended up going to that open gym alone that day to play basketball. It was me and seven other guys there. I would say the average age was nineteen. I hurt for a week after playing just four pickup basketball games. It was awesome. Do things that set you apart from the crowd. Being unique is a GOOD thing, especially when your brand of uniqueness is *healthier and stronger than everyone else here.*

Remember, the goal, in part, is for her to be able to point at you from across the room and proudly say, *"That's MY man right there."*

I'm sorry, your "dad bod" doesn't cut it. It's called a "dad bod" for a reason. All dads have it. It's boring. It's typical. You look like a salamander. You're a cliché, a joke among women.

Your dad bod screams comfort. It screams, *"I ain't going anywhere."* Not because you are faithful and reliable, mind you, but because you CAN'T go anywhere. You have no choice. No other woman lusts after you. That's precisely why women SAY they like dad bods. It gives them a sense of comfort and it makes them feel better about their own lazy and aging bodies.

Yes, many women do claim to absolutely LOVE the typical dad bod. When questioned as to what makes the dad bod so attractive, they will often say: *"I can't have a guy that looks better than me. That's just wrong."* Translation: *"If my man was super hot, I would constantly worry about every other woman salivating over him. I have to be assured that I'm not going to lose my mate."*

As I have often said, a relationship with obviously mismatched attraction levels is NOT sustainable. Your wife knows this; every woman knows this.

The typical dad bod may make them feel more comfortable about themselves, but it doesn't make them want you sexually. There's a huge difference between the two states of mind.

Remember, if no other woman wants you, then your wife probably doesn't want you, either.

After you get in shape, other men will notice you being different from the pack (attractive) right away. They may try to avoid you. When you do chat, they will be more submissive. When their wives are around, they will be more aggressive and protective. You will hear men saying things to make you look weaker and inferior around their wives. Their wives aren't stupid. They will pick up on this right away. The man's stupid "mate guarding" tactics will backfire and will end up just making you look more attractive. You want to be the kind of guy that other men feel nervous leaving their wives alone with.

You'll discover that your newfound physical fitness will make your wife nervous and worried. You'll notice more jealousy pop up here and there. She may even get angry at your new fitness hobby. She may have a genuine hissy fit about it. You may tell her that you're no longer eating sweets or snacking between meals, and the next thing you know she has baked your favorite cake and she bought three bags of Chex-Mix, your favorite salty snack, and she put them right next to the coffee machine, so you'll see them first thing in the morning on your way to work.

Yes, she is sabotaging your efforts. She wants you to fail; she doesn't want you to succeed. That can be heartbreaking to many men who had hoped that their wife would be their biggest cheerleader in their new fitness quest. Instead, she's his biggest opponent.

That's probably more common than not, to be honest. Things are changing and she doesn't like it. She is not at ease.

THIS IS A GOOD THING. DON'T FIGHT IT. STAY THE COURSE.

Welcome to being an attractive dude. It comes with drama. A lot of anxious men make a mistake at this point: They freak out when their wives get stressed and angry about their positive changes, and then they explain everything away. They tell their wives how they wanted to turn their sex lives around, so they started going to the gym. They talk about the books they read and the YouTube videos they watched. They share their favorite marriage podcast.

"No no, mommy. Please don't be mad! I was just trying to do things for YOU!"

WRONG WRONG WRONG.

Your newfound level of fitness and confidence is NOT just for her and your sex life but for YOU. If you even hint at this being for HER and that you're just trying to improve your sex life, you will go from being sexy to pitiful in a nanosecond.

You're still the nice but creepy guy doing things for mommy's affection. She's still up on the proverbial pedestal. She's still the boss.

Your self-improvement is for YOURSELF. The consequences of your self-improvement MAY be more sex from your wife, but sex should never be the overt intention. It sounds stupid… but your woman wants a natural, not a guy who tries out different things to win her love and affection again. What's the difference between you and a natural? There is none. There's no such thing as a natural. Everyone learns. Whether you are a "natural" or not is all in their perception. If you do something with little effort and do it with no ulterior motive or attention-seeking in mind, you are a "natural."

You just keep taking care of yourself, looking better, and getting healthier. No explaining. No rationalizing. No approval-seeking. Make it a natural, normal part of your life… because that's precisely what it should be.

Going to the gym, lifting weights, gaining muscle, and losing fat is the first step towards turning things around. It's the first and probably the most impactful step, to be honest. For some men, they can stop right here, and their bedroom situation will improve tremendously. The physical and mental improvements that come with regular physical exercise cannot be overstated.

Just watch. Your hard work may inspire your wife to get HER ass back in the gym, too. She may start throwing away the snacks. She may start sharing her favorite fitness podcast with you. It's funny how that works.

Couples that are completely mismatched in attraction levels are rare. Unless, of course, we're talking about the Super-Provider man and his beautiful trophy wife. We all know about that couple and how that story ends.

Think about it. How many times have you seen a super handsome guy with a homely, overweight wife? Exactly. Your wife knows that is not a sustainable relationship dynamic. Watch her as she instinctively kicks up her own fitness a few notches and starts pointing out her improvements.

"I think my belly looks a little smaller. Don't you?"

She knows she must compete with a lot more women now.
This is a very good thing. Don't you dare go and try and
out-nice this instinctive reaction. Believe it or not, your
wife is enjoying this new change. She enjoys having to play
catch-up with her husband who seems to be hell-bent on
getting in amazing shape. She actually LIKES that little bit
of anxiety and pressure that she's experiencing. It's been a
long time since she's looked up to you in this way.
Enjoy it.

Be Her Lover Step #2: Go Away

The Lover is scarce. He has other things to do. What things? Well, that's not too clear. He may be working hard, doing some hobby, going out with friends… or possibly out seeing other women.

He's not always available for a quick chat. He doesn't always divulge his whereabouts or plans. He does not anxiously overshare. He has a date with his girl planned for Saturday, and she may not hear a peep from him until then. This drives his women crazy, which can be a good thing. The Lover unknowingly taps into a big secret of attraction. Part of the libido-sucking nature of a long-term, monogamous relationship is tied to familiarity and comfort. You can call it "relationship fatigue."

"Oh… it's you again. Great."

You're always there. You're dependable. She just has to say, *"Honey?!"* and you'll be by her side in a nanosecond.

This may sound like what a true "life partner" is supposed to be, but it absolutely kills the typical female sexual desire.

"Familiarity breeds contempt."
"Absence makes the heart grow fonder."

Have you heard these sayings before? Of course you have. These axioms didn't just fall from the sky. They've been around for generations for a reason: they're true!

The natural progression of a typical long-term, monogamous relationship includes the initial honeymoon phase, then the fun awkwardness of learning about each other's quirks, blemishes, and vices, and then the stress and boredom as you concentrate on keeping the household/parenting machine running as smoothly as possible.

As the relationship timeline progresses, the time spent together increases. It's no coincidence that the frequency of sex also goes down at this phase.

Simply put, you need to frequently get away from your wife. You need time for YOU. Contrary to popular belief, there is nothing wrong with alone time. It doesn't make you a substandard father or husband. As a matter of fact, it does quite the opposite: It makes you a more well-rounded and mentally healthy human being.

Get active. When you are on the couch day after day, your wife's inner cavewoman programming says, "Aren't you supposed to be out chasing sabretooth tigers and getting us some food or something?" This is precisely why the napping husband seems to piss women off so much.

Be energetic. Don't let life beat you down and wear you out so easily. Get out there and tackle the world.

Trust me, as a father of four who works full-time, I totally understand the desire to just say, "Fuck it," and relax at home. It's perfectly okay to take a timeout on a regular basis to recalibrate, but it's not okay to do this day after day after day.

Get away from your wife. Go do things for YOU.

Yes, being away from her may increase her anxiety and cause her some worry. But that's okay, your initial dating life—the "honeymoon phase"—was fraught with such anxiety:

- "Does he like me?"

- "Does he not like me?"

- "Is he tired of me already?"

- "Am I too fat?"

- "Does he respect me?"

- "Oh my god, did I really just say that?"

- "Does this outfit look too slutty?"

- "Does he think I'm stupid?"

- "Is he dating other girls?"

- "Did that girl just look at him? Did he look back? Does he know her?"

It sounds exhausting and torturous (welcome to the world

of the way-more neurotic female mind), but here's what's interesting: That anxiety is a crucial ingredient for what sparked her early relationship libido in the first place. It sounds counterintuitive, but those feelings she had weren't necessarily a bad thing. They meant she cared and was invested in growing your relationship. SHE WAS TURNED ON. She was in the beginning stages of being "in love."

The opposite of being in love is not hate, it's indifference. When you see each other day after day, that anxiety is gone. The drama is gone. She becomes indifferent. She knows where you are at all times. She knows what each day is going to bring. Life is all mapped out for her.

She's bored.

Nothing good comes from a bored wife. Ever. She will eventually seek excitement elsewhere. That doesn't necessarily mean she will start banging the neighbor guy, but it does often result in a wife who does things that pull her farther away from her safe and predictable mate. She will seek out other sources for the much-needed dopamine hit that got her hooked on you to begin with. You're not immune to this phenomenon either, by the way. Lots of you guys routinely watch porn, gamble, or visit sex workers.

Drama. Anxiety. Feelings. Excitement. These are the foundation of the female libido. Yes, we men like our dopamine hits, too… but we have this thing called "an excessive amount of testosterone" that keeps our sexual desire at a pretty consistent level, even when our lives are insanely predictable and boring. Your wife is NOT the same.

Embrace the newfound drama and anxiety. Don't run from it. Drama is your friend. It means you're doing something right.

It's okay for her to be a little anxious. Stop trying to alleviate her stress all the time, especially when that stress is indicative of a normal and healthy male-female relationship. Sometimes the emotional tension can be a very positive thing.

Stop fearing her negativity. Stop with the *"okay, okay, okay… I'll do whatever you want"* attitude you've had all these years. Your wife wants a man who can take her drama and laugh it off. Remember, the myth of *"happy wife equals happy life"*? Stop tiptoeing around her. Let her be anxious and upset. It's okay.

REMEMBER THIS: YOU'RE DOING NOTHING WRONG.

You're simply getting out of the house and taking care of yourself. You're trying to better yourself as a man. Bravo to you.

Do you have any "player" type of friends who are dating lots of women? Ask them about female drama. Sit back in awe as he shares crazy story after crazy story.
The player gets frequent sex. With sex comes drama. With

drama comes sex. He's well aware of this dynamic. He doesn't care. He has a harem of seven different girls he can call on for fun. When Sally gets a little too crazy, he ignores her and calls Debra instead. All the women know about each other. This causes more drama… and consequently more sex for him.

Sounds exhausting, doesn't it? Luckily, you have just one drama queen to contend with.

You need time to yourself, even if/when it results in anxiety and drama from your wife. Getting away is healthy. It's good for your mental health. It's good for your growth as a human being. You need to discover more of yourself again. Your wife probably needs to do the same. Encourage her to do solo activities, as well.

REMEMBER, things that make you a better man = things that help to create an environment for your wife's sexual desire to grow.

You can't become a better dude if you are constantly by your wife's side. She doesn't hold all the tools to make you a more complete man. Yes, she's your partner and mom to your kid, but she's also a girl. Girls and boys don't do well after being together for long periods, in case you didn't notice.

No, hiding in your "man cave" doesn't count. That's just your little designated area of the house. You're still in the house and still with your wife. You need to get out and do your own thing. Get away from her. Get out of your comfort zone. Expand your horizons.

Trust me, she doesn't need you around all the time. She's a big girl and can take care of things for a little while.

Men should welcome the idea of going out on their own. It should be a relief. You should look forward to it. My dad used to go to the hardware store for four hours at a time. He wasn't buying anything (because who really needs to be at the hardware store for FOUR HOURS?!). He was drinking coffee, eating popcorn, and "shooting the shit with the boys" while looking at tools and planning his next home project. He needed the time away to recalibrate after being around a kid and wife for so many hours a day.

This is normal and healthy behavior for a man.

You Need a Mission

For every man, I recommend that you get a "mission" in life, something very specific to shoot for. You need to set a goal or a series of goals; you need a purpose in life outside of your family. You need to create a series of steps to reach that goal. You do those steps a little at a time. Along the way of reaching your goal, you attain little "quick wins" that give your brain and body the boost it needs to keep going. After much hard work and determination, you reach the end goal, only to find that another goal immediately appears in the distance.

This is called being a "man on a mission." This, my friend, is the secret to a fulfilling life.

I can't stress enough how important this is. I can't stress enough how this MUST be something that is geared towards YOU and your interests and falls outside of the realm of the family. In other words, "I'm going to coach my kid's baseball team to a championship" is not a mission. "I'm going to save up money and take my family to Hawaii" is not a mission.

These are examples of missions:

1. *"I've always wanted to pursue art and sculpting more. I'm going to take classes at the nearby art school. I'm going to mentor with somebody and learn. I'm going to attend my first art show. I'm going to sell my first piece. I'm going to be in the big art gallery in town. Eventually, people all over the world will buy my sculptures through my website."*

2. *"I'm going to start a charity for homeless veterans in my city. I'm going to contact some other homeless veteran charities in other cities to see what it is they are doing to combat the problem. I'm going to learn all I can about mental health. I'm going to talk to struggling veterans to get an idea of what life is like for them. I'm going to put a plan down on paper. I'm going to learn about fundraising. I'm going to open a shelter for homeless veterans in my city... maybe in other cities, as well."*

3. *"I'm going to get in the best shape of my life and start a website chronicling my journey. I'm going to learn all I can*

about diet and exercise and share my results along the way. I'm going to interview experts in the field like doctors and trainers. I'm going to start a podcast about my journey. I'm eventually going to have companies ask to sponsor my site and podcast. I'm going to make this a legitimate second source of income. I'm going to look like a male fitness model and be an inspiration to millions of other normal guys who want to do the same."

When men have a very real mission for life, the act of "getting away" and doing what they can to better themselves as men… that kind of takes care of itself. You'll find yourself hanging out and learning from a growing group of new people you call friends. You find that you're not so caught up in your wife's day-to-day emotions and therefore you're not so needy at home. You'll find, for once, that your wife is the one fighting for YOUR attention and affection. This is normal. This is the dynamic that a woman is typically more comfortable in.

Welcome to being a mentally healthy man.

Your wife wants to be in the position of having to earn the attention and affection of a man on a mission. She wants to tell people that her guy is "just so busy" doing cool and important things. When you and your wife do get together for alone time, it should be an event. It should be a fun and sexy break from the domestic life that does such a good job of smothering sexuality and desire.

Get out. Do things. Be a better and more rounded

man. Your wife, and your life in general, will thank you.

NOTE: We have a private group for men only called the HFM Brotherhood, which you may find helpful in your journey. We have very active private discussion forums, a members-only podcast, live Zoom meetings (all of them are recorded in case you miss one), access to all of my books at no additional charge, and access to in-person conferences and meetups. We also have our coaching and courses available at big discounts. Working with other men who are on the same journey can drastically help expedite your efforts. Go to helpformen.com/join to learn more.

Be Her Lover Step #3: Be Unique

In every romantic relationship, we want to believe that the person we picked is different from the rest of the pack. We want to believe that our partner possesses a unique, unicorn level of awesomeness that cannot be equaled by anyone else. We want to believe they are extremely scarce and in high demand.

"They are so awesome AND they chose ME?!"

Similarly, you want to portray to your partner that yes, they made the right choice in picking you as well. You are also a rare find among a giant population of losers; their efforts were not in vain.

"I'm not like other women." Every woman in a relationship has said this. Every single one. They know how important it is to stand out from the pack if they want to achieve peak attractiveness. They know what nutcases many women are and how unattractive that is.

"I'm not like other women… I like hanging out with guys more," is another common statement women give. They feel it gives them a leg up over the competition. Makes them more trustworthy. It actually does the opposite—a woman who hangs out mostly with men is sometimes a relationship red flag.

SIDE NOTE: Many men emailed me after reading the above statement in previous editions of this book, asking me to expand on this further. (Apparently, a lot of men have heard the "I like hanging out with guys more" line from their wives.) As with all red flags, this doesn't necessarily signify "DANGER, YOUR WIFE IS CHEATING ON YOU." It just means that it is something to be aware of and to watch carefully. To quote from my third book, RED FLAGS:

"'I just like hanging out with guys more. They're way less drama.'

We've all heard this a time or two in our lives. Loosely translated, this means, 'The attention I get from the opposite sex makes me feel special. The fact that I can manipulate and dominate a relationship via my sexuality is a very good thing for me. These types of relationships always work in my favor. Strictly platonic relationships where there is no implied sexuality or exchange of favors are of no use to me. I just feel inadequate when I am in a relationship with equals.'"

Ask a woman about the man she's crazy in love with (usually early in the relationship) and she will jump immediately into what sets him apart from the rest. She may mention his job and that he's a really sweet guy… but not until she gets out of the way exactly WHY she devotes so much energy to this guy:

"He's really cute. He's into art. He does his own sculptures out of glass and wood. He also plays in a band on some weekends."

You need to stick out from the rest of the pack. Don't blend in. Don't follow the standard script that so many other dads do. Don't be the mopey, boring, dad bod, no style, watch football, take kids to soccer, take out the trash, go to bed, go to work kinda guy. If you just sit back, watch, and emulate what everybody else does, you'll just end up getting what everybody else gets: a boring, non-sexual relationship. Be interesting. Be different.

Uniqueness is an important ingredient for her delicate sex drive soufflé. She craves different. She craves special. She craves unique.

The same ol' same ol' is BORING. Remember, don't let your wife get bored!

Let's look at this from a more scientific angle. For a woman to devote herself to just YOU and only YOU is a really big deal for her. She does not take it lightly. Ideally, she wants to pick one REALLY GOOD man to stick with for a long time. Because… what if she gets pregnant? She's then stuck with this guy and his offspring for YEARS.

This man she has chosen better be healthy, smart, tough… an all-around good dude. Not only does he need to pass on his great, healthy man genes to the baby, but he also needs to stick around to help take care of her and the kid. Even if the woman has zero interest in children or is past her baby-making years, she still has this baseline instinctual drive. It is the basis for all female attraction (in hetero relationships).

Remember: Lover + Provider = Ideal man

If he's not that kind of guy, then she has made a giant, life-changing mistake. Unfortunately, most guys are NOT that kind of guy. At all. Ask any woman who has been single for a while. It's scary how bad their pool of male candidates is.

Therefore, the kind of guy they want is "different" from the rest of that pitiful pack of candidates out there. The good news is that it doesn't take much to be better than all these poor saps who are out there trying to get laid.

When her brain feels, "He's different and worthy of my attention," that's a crucial step towards turning the sexual engine on.

"I don't know why, but I like you."

Why do you think the skinny, androgynous rock star makes women so weak in the knees? He's literally UP ON THE PEDESTAL of the stage, away from the rest of the plebes. Lights are shining on him. He's the most important person in the building at that moment. He's confident. He looks like a total weirdo, but he doesn't care. He has little to no anxiety in the moment. He is the epitome of confidence.
Everyone can see him. Everyone can hear him. He can do whatever and their eyes will follow. Women stare in awe,

put their hands to their faces, and scream. It's all just too much to take in.

The rock star is about as different, unique, interesting, and stand-out-from-the-pack as you can get. It's not about his money, either. Ask any single guy who started up a garage band and started doing gigs for $500 on weekends. He rarely went back home without a girl on his arm. It's like shooting fish in a barrel for him.

Him: *"I play guitar for the band."*

Her: *"Oh, reeeeaaally? That's so awesome!"* [twirling her hair]

To further illustrate the importance of being unique, are you familiar with the world of "pickup artists"? It's a hilarious and extremely interesting subculture of socially awkward men (dorks) who discovered that their success rate of "picking up" women can be dramatically improved by doing and saying very specific things at just the right time.

They're basically some nerds who studied women like lab rats and watched how they behaved in certain conditions. They saw which actions created interest and which didn't. They saw which actions resulted in getting the woman's number and which actions resulted in getting ignored or a drink thrown in their faces. They treated women as if they were math problems.
Obviously, the pickup artist is not too popular with women or society in general. Nobody likes being treated like a lab

rat. Nobody likes a fraud who learned how to fake being charming. Nobody likes some weirdo who is pretending to be a certain person just to get into a girl's pants. That's very fake and very creepy.

Again, we all like "naturals."

With that being said, a lot of what the pickup artists teach actually works. It's sometimes forced, contrived, and completely cringe-worthy, but if they do everything right, they achieve their goal: They get laid way more often than they did before. Morals aside, that's a win in their book.

One important concept the pickup artists push is called "peacocking." Picture a peacock fanning his feathers open and strutting around in front of a peahen. He's saying, *"Does this bountiful and colorful plumage set me apart from the rest? I have some GOOD genes here, girlfriend. I make very healthy babies."*

Peacocking is the same in humans. You must visually set yourself apart from the flock. You could be a muscular Adonis with a chiseled jaw and pecs bulging out of your shirt… or you could wear something flamboyant and ridiculous that makes women stop and go, *"What the…?"* It may be a leopard print coat, a giant fuzzy hat, painted nails… whatever. It's admittedly ridiculous, but all this peacocking has a purpose. It says:

"I'm unique. Plus, I really don't give a shit what other people think about me. I am a low-anxiety, high-confidence man.

I don't recommend walking around with a toilet plunger stuck to your head and a glowing set of pink nipple rings while at home with your wife… but the underlying concept is valid. Stick out somehow. Don't give a shit what everyone else thinks. Don't be needy. Don't be anxious. Be confident. Be unique.

Do something that makes her say, *"Yep… I picked a good one. He's different than the rest of you assholes."*

Some ideas:

- Take a dance class.
- Take up a form of art like painting, sculpting, or photography.
- Learn a martial art, like Jiu Jitsu.
- Coach your kid's sports team.
- Start up a charity.
- Write a book.
- Play an instrument.
- Take an acting class.

At this point in the book, what should now be starting to click in your brain is that all of this is not a "trick." It's not "manipulation." It's work. It's called "being a better man." Remember: Things that make you a better man are things that help create the environment that allows your wife's sexual desire to grow.

Be Her Lover Step #4: You Must Lead and Set the Tone of the Relationship

A guy reaches out to me for a coaching session. His chief complaint is he's not getting anywhere near the amount of sex he wants from his wife. He does what most men do in these conversations: He starts to list off his various Provider traits as proof of his worth. He works hard, he's a great dad, he buys things for his wife, he has been faithful (even though he had "some easy opportunities to cheat in the past"—all men point this out to me for some reason), he doesn't flirt with other women, he helps around the house and with the kids a lot, etc.

Me: *"Okay... but what do you do that is SEXY?"*

Him: *"What do you mean?"*

Me: *"You know... what do you do to set the mood? How do you let her know you love her, find her attractive, and want her sexually?"*

Him: *"I tell her.*

Me: *"What do you tell her?"*

Him: *"That I love her."*

Me: *"Well... you tell your kids you love them. That's not*

sexy. How do you go from that to sexy?"

Him: *"I'll give her massages and stuff when we go to bed sometimes. She really likes that. Then I ask her if she feels like having sex. She usually says no. Oh, and sometimes we go out to dinner, just the two of us, when my parents can watch the kids. Go to the movies... stuff like that. I don't know what else to do."*

Wow... how does she keep her hands off of you, Casa Nova?

This is so very typical for men. Guys thinking like guys. They think it's a 4-step process.

1. Lie down next to wife.

2. Give her a massage or an overt sexual signal (like grabbing her boob).

3. Say you love her.

4. Ask for sex.

No.

Remember... this is a delicate soufflé. This isn't a firecracker you just light and watch explode. This is a recipe that has lots of ingredients. Baking this soufflé takes TIME... and patience.

I know, when you first started dating your wife, you two were all over each other (at least I hope so). All you had to do was walk in the door and she was ready to go, sometimes several times per day! Well, that was the ol' honeymoon phase, my friend. Things, in case you can't tell, are a little different now. To get a glimpse of that girlfriend you fell in love with is going to take WORK.

It is up to you to set the tone of sexiness in the relationship. If you sit back and wait for your wife to initiate sex without ANY action on your part, you will be one frustrated dude. I know this is a common ploy by a lot of angry guys in dead-bedroom marriages: *"I'm going to stop chasing her and see what she does."* I can save you the time. It's not going to work. She'll just be happy that you got off her back for once.

Putting in the work and initiating doesn't mean massaging her and saying, "Let's fuck." It means being way more subtle, genuine, and consistent over a longer period of time.

Here are some examples of small actions you can do over the next few months to set the proper tone (NOTE: These ideas will only work if you have your physicality and mindset in line. Do all of the other steps first):

1. When you walk by your wife at home, give her a little brush and squeeze with your hand. Just a little something to say, *"I'm here… I see you there, sexy girl. I appreciate you."* Nothing more. Just the little squeeze of the arm or shoulder. A hand on the small of her back. No words.

2. Walking behind her while she cooks? Give her a smooch on the back of her head. Tell her she looks

beautiful. Tell her how much you love and appreciate her. Thank her for that thing she did earlier in the day. Walk away. Nothing else.

3. She's carrying a load of laundry? Grab it from her. *"Here babe, I got it."* As you reach for the basket, pull her in and give her a smooch. Say to her, "You look really good today." Leave it at that.

4. She's getting ready in the morning in front of the bedroom mirror? Give her butt a squeeze and say, *"Mmmm. That's what I like right there."* Walk away. Nothing more.

You're giving little gifts of love and affection. It's part of setting the sexy tone. With those brief little touches, kisses, and compliments, you're reminding your wife that she's more than just a mom. She's a woman. She's a sexual person. You are setting the stage for genuine connection. You are telling her that you're still a COUPLE and not just Mom and Dad. You are NOT doing these things because you expect sex from her. In fact, you don't care if she reciprocates your affection or not. She may be frustrated at times with your touches and bluntly say, "NO SEX TONIGHT!" That's cool with you. You just smile and joke with her: "Wow… pervert. Who said anything about sex?" Or a smile, a simple "Okay" and a quick change of topic will do.

Outcome should never be on your mind when it comes to these little signs of connection. They're just a genuine expression of your love and appreciation for your wife.

Her little verbal jabs should just bounce right off of you. This is crucial for setting the right tone in the relationship. You don't give two shits if your actions result in sex or not. Your feelings are not so easily hurt by her. You are not so emotionally dependent upon her reaction to you and what you do.

> (Note: Little verbal jabs from your wife CAN later become real toxic asshole behavior. Context is everything. If she's being offensive or disrespectful for no damn reason, let her know right then and there. Don't wait. Call her out on it. Yes, drama will ensue, but that's okay. The alternative is that you train her to think that insulting her man and being an asshole is perfectly acceptable.)

You're the man. You love her; you appreciate her. She doesn't want to reciprocate your little positive moments right then and there? Meh… no biggy. Who knows what's going on in her head at the moment. Maybe you just caught her at a bad time. You're not doing these things to get mommy's approval. You're doing them because you're a loving, sexual creature.

She's a woman. You're a man. You are awesome together. These very brief, little gifts of attention are reminders of that.

You need to present an aura that says:

"I'm sexy…I love you… here, let me give you a little smooch to remind you of how much you mean to me. Now I need to go

do something else. I'm a busy, unique, and valuable man."

Just like regular gift-giving and chores, you do these little things because you WANT to do them. You do them from a genuine mindset of *"I really don't give a shit if you do anything in return or not."*

You're projecting an image of high value, confidence, sexiness, and lustfulness without a hint of neediness or expectation of reward. This is extremely important to internalize.
Neediness should never be the foundation of your love and affection. All it does is put more pressure and stress on your wife. Sex with you should not be a chore or a requirement of her as your wife, but instead, it should be a natural progression of your already sexual and fun relationship. It's just the normal and expected next step in the process of how you show love and affection to each other.

With the needy husband gone, the negative pressure is lifted from your wife's shoulders. She suddenly has one less kid in the house. She has a man, a sexy man who still has desire for her even after all these months/years of being neglected. Combine this loving aloofness with your new gym body, your independence, and your unique qualities that set you apart from the rest... and eventually she'll start to feel that little twitch in the back of her mind. That's when her brain starts churning away with all those estrogen-fueled thoughts:

"What was that about? That was sweet of him. Why did he

do that? I should've kissed him back. Does he still expect sex? I really don't feel like it. When was the last time we had sex? I bet he's just doing that for sex. I get tired of his whining. Where's he going? He did that this morning, too. He hasn't asked me for sex in a while. Maybe he found somebody else. No way. Could be… I mean, I saw how that woman at work was flirting with him. I don't even think he noticed… or maybe he did notice and they're having a secret affair and he tried to act all innocent. He has been going to the gym more. He looks better than I do. I bet he thinks I'm gross. I have a horrible mom body. I should go to yoga with Sally. Wait, was that a new shirt he had on? When did he buy that? Maybe his mistress bought it for him. Oh my god… is this a midlife crisis? Suzy's husband left her for that young secretary last year. No way my husband would do that, though. Or would he? That would be so embarrassing for me and terrible for the kids. Everyone will think I was too ugly for him. I bet he's totally cheating. What if he isn't? Am I a terrible wife?"

Exhausting to read, but does it look familiar? This is similar to the anxiety she felt at the beginning of your relationship. This is the little natural twinge of worry that so many guys try to squash immediately. But you're smart. You're different. You know this is a good thing. This means she's starting to feel attraction towards you again. You let her brain do its thing and you just keep being the best and most attractive guy you can be.

There's nothing you can do to stop her brain from spinning a mile a minute. Nor do you want to.

"But, she's going to think I'm cheating on her!"

And? So what? ARE you really cheating on her? NO. You're simply being the awesome guy that so many other women in her shoes would KILL to have at home. That's why she's so anxious. It's not because you're doing anything wrong. You're not at all. You're doing everything RIGHT. That puts pressure on her. This reintroduces feelings she hasn't experienced in quite a while.

You're making progress.

Repeat after me: You're doing nothing wrong.

STOP FEELING SO DAMN SHAMEFUL ABOUT BEING A BETTER MAN.

You're a good man doing good things to attempt to reignite your wife's desire for you… so that you two can continue staying together in a happy marriage—just like you promised to do in your vows on your wedding day.

Wow. How horrible. You manipulative monster. How do you live with yourself?

It's shortly after her brain spins out of control that she will decide to consult with a friend or two about your situation.

Here's how a typical friend conversation will go:

Wife: *"I'm worried about Steve. He's not acting right."*

Friend: *"What's going on?"*

Wife: *"I think he's having a midlife crisis."*

Friend: *"Oh no! What's he doing?"*

Wife: *"He lost some weight… started going to the gym. He's dressing all young and sexy now. It's very weird."*

Friend: *"Oh no… that's how Suzy's husband acted before he left her and the kids. Remember?"*

Wife: *"Yeah, I know. That's why I'm worried."*

Friend: *"Does he act like he hates you now? Ignores you? Starts fights for no reason?"*

Wife: *"No, not at all. He's been very sweet lately. Loving. Gives me kisses all the time. He grabs my butt and stuff more now. Calls me beautiful. Helps out more around the house. Tells me how much he appreciates me."*

Friend: *"Oh, well … that sounds perfect. What's the problem here?! He sounds like Sara's husband, Joe. He's great to her. They're probably the happiest couple I know. She just got boob implants last week. She says they were a gift to him… to keep him away from the young girls. Ha! They just went on a cruise last month. You should see their* pictures. They both look really good for their age."

Wife: "Yeah, I'm not getting boob implants anytime soon! I dunno… Maybe I'm overreacting. It makes me realize what a bitch I've been for a while. He's doing all these things… and he doesn't ask anything of me, ever. We also haven't had sex in a while. He stopped pressuring me."

Friend: "Oh really? That's not good. How long has it been since you had sex?"

Wife: "I dunno… weeks? Maybe months?"

Friend: "Oh, sweetie… that's not good. And he's not asking for it? A man can't go on that long without sex. He's going to explode. That's what happened with Suzy's husband. They had the baby, and she didn't want sex anymore. He got a new girlfriend almost immediately and filed for divorce."

Wife: "I know. Trust me, I get it. It doesn't help that other women are staring at him all the time. He's so clueless he doesn't even notice. He took his shirt off and was showing off his new abs the other day when he washed the car outside in the driveway. I think Karen next door just about had a heart attack. Even her husband was staring."

Friend: "Steve has abs now?! Wow. I didn't know that. My husband hasn't been in good shape since…ever. Good for you, girlfriend! You got a hotty for a husband! You really need to take care of him, then! If you won't, trust me… somebody else will!"

Wife: *"Yeah, I guess. I should probably get my flabby ass back in the gym, then. Haha."*

Friend: *"Yeah. Wow…I mean, no! You look great. I knew Steve was looking really good lately but didn't know he was in THAT good shape."*

Wife: *"Alright, don't you start drooling, too! This is my husband we're talking about!"*

Friend: *"I know! You're a lucky girl. It may not last! I'd be enjoying it if I were you."*

Notice how she went from, *"I'm worried about his weird behavior,"* to, *"Yeah, I guess I am lucky and should get my ass in the gym instead of whining"*? You think this conversation sounds made up or far-fetched? Hell no. This is a very realistic example of what could happen when your wife starts getting anxious about your changes.

1. Wife is worried about new-husband behavior.

2. She doesn't know quite how to process so she confers with peer group.

3. Peer group digests information and points out that her husband is attractive to others and loving. This is good and she should shape her ass up.

4. She agrees to shape her ass up and stop whining about

nothing.

A lot of guys, myself included, really don't understand why their wife needs to check in with their social group all the time to confirm what is so obvious to us. I used to get REALLY upset with my ex-wife for checking in with her peer group about every little thing I would say or do. For one, I saw it as a lack of respect towards me (it was)… and two, it made me feel less respect for her. What kind of adult needs to check in with people all the time to form an opinion about things that are so basic?

It could be about the absolute dumbest things:

Me: *"No, sweetie. You don't want to pour that bacon grease down the drain. It can clog the pipes and it's no good for the sewer. Just put it in the trash can."*

Ex-wife: *"No, I'm pretty sure you can pour it down the drain."* [continues pouring grease down the drain]

Me: *"No, just dump it in the trash. Please."*

[Next day]

Ex-wife: *"I talked to Brenda at work and she says you shouldn't put bacon grease down the drain."*

Me: *"Oh, good. I'm glad you checked in with Brenda, The Queen of Bacon Grease and Master Plumber Extraordinaire... Or you could just listen to your husband*

You must come to terms with the fact that much of how your wife feels and how she processes things about you and your relationship is largely determined by her peer group. If you do something that pisses off her best friend Sally, you damn well better believe that Sally will let your wife know ASAP and not let up until your wife does something about it.

Conversely, if you do something that Sally thinks is amazing… your wife will also hear about it. Sally gushing over you will win you A LOT of attraction points. Sally's pushing the buttons for you. That's a very good thing. The lesson is that women are very social creatures. They are very high in what psychologists call "trait openness." They want both direction and acceptance from their peer group. They want reassurance. Your wife WILL take Sally's advice and perspective to heart, and it will affect your marriage— positively or negatively. That's just the way it is.

What you want to do is set the tone of the relationship so that it minimizes the impact of stupid, negative outside influencers like Sally. You want to become an undeniably good thing. You want to become the guy who repeatedly pushes her buttons. You want to become the husband that the other wives can't wait to hear stories about. You want your wife to be your number one fan. That is when your wife sees herself as part of your TEAM, rather than the stressed-out wife who constantly complains about her husband. When she's part of your team, it's you two against the rest of the world.

That's when you do your best as a couple. That's when your wife will be happiest… as your co-captain in life.

Get Her Away from the Kids

As I have said many times in my writing, parenthood is the antithesis of eroticism. The two worlds do not mesh. As far as "major turnoffs" are concerned, being a parent is right up around the top of the list (along with global pandemics, job loss, and farting husbands).

When your wife is in MOM mode, she is ONLY in mom mode.

Many men make the mistake of trying to introduce overt sexuality into situations where it just doesn't belong. Here are some common examples. Any of these sound familiar?

1. The wife is busy wiping up baby vomit and the husband reaches down and gives her dangling, sore mom boob a squeeze. He seems genuinely perplexed and hurt when she yells, "CAN YOU PLEASE NOT DO THAT?!"

2. The wife just finished yelling at the fifteen-year-old for the hundredth time about stupid things the dumb teen keeps insisting on doing. The wife looks like she has been to hell and back. Dad looks at his wife sympathetically and says, "So… *you wanna do it tonight? We didn't get around to doing it last week like we said we would.*" She turns around and goes into the other room without saying a word.

3. Mom got a call from the school. The nine-year-old got into a fight and broke the other kid's nose. The wife is

very upset. She sobs and says that she can't believe her son is a "bully" and would do something like that. Husband assures her that it is no big deal, boys fight sometimes, and besides, *"I'll make you feel all better tonight in the bathtub."* The wife immediately looks up at the husband with tears streaming down her face: *"What the fuck is wrong with you?"*

When it comes to getting your wife in the right headspace for sexuality, it's all about CONTEXT. You need to learn to read the room. You need to learn when and where it is a good time to be sexy, and when it's time to back off and play the part of concerned friend.

Once you have kids, this part of the husband job gets exponentially more difficult.

Simply put, having children is a short-cut method to ruining your sex life. I know, it sounds terrible, but it's true. I can't tell you how many men have told me that sex with their wife ceased after their new baby came into the world. As a client of mine said to me once, *"I can understand how sexual intimacy dies down during the first year or so after the kid is born... but not twenty years later!"*

Simply put, the wife's body and brain shift gears completely once she becomes a mother. "MOM MODE: ENGAGED. MUST PROTECT CHILDREN. EVERYTHING ELSE COMES SECOND TO CHILDREN. FORGET HUSBAND."

Many men believe that this was an evil and manipulative

bait-and-switch routine on the wife's part. She just needed him to procreate. Once the baby came out, she was free to shut down the sex life that she was never really into to begin with. I'm sure that happens from time to time, but the more realistic and less sinister truth is that she really DID want frequent sex with her husband during the pre-kid, honeymoon stage of their marriage, but under the pressure of being a new parent, the world of sexuality is now completely smothered. What used to come "naturally" now takes "work"… and as any parent will tell you, adding more "work" to your to-do list sounds like the last thing you want to do.

For MANY couples, if you want to grow closer together and increase your chances of intimacy, you need to get away from the world of parenthood as much as humanly possible. You need to do so on a regular basis. Date nights are a must, but that is the minimum. You need weekends away. You need to leave the kids with grandma and grandpa, aunts and uncles, and friends… and go away together on an adventure as a couple.

I always tell men to plan a surprise trip without telling the wife about any of the details. Arrange all of the logistics needed to make the trip happen. Arrange for childcare. Plan the trip. Pay for everything upfront. Play the part of the leader. Your wife should come home from work and see a husband sitting on the couch with a suitcase next to him.

You: *"Welcome home, beautiful. You have one hour to get ready. You and I are going on a trip. Bring a bathing suit, one nice dress for going out for dinner, and lots of casual clothes for hiking. We will be gone for three days. Everything is planned for and taken care of.”*

Her: *“Uhhhh… what? What about the kids? Billy has baseball tomorrow and I have to work on that project with Sally. Remember?”*

You: *“As I said, all taken care of. The kids are handled. Trust me. Everything has been planned. All you have to worry about is relaxing and enjoying a fun trip with your husband. Now, I suggest you hurry… you have fifty-five minutes left to get ready.”*

A lot of men will try some semblance of the "surprise trip" and get angry as their wife throws every protest imaginable at him. *"I'm trying to be an awesome husband for her! Why is she such a bitch about it!?"*

You can think of this reaction from her as a type of shit test. Let it bounce off of you. Of course she is going to protest; of course she is going to be anxious. You just threw a giant left turn into her life and disrupted her routine.

She's a typical stressed-out mom. She must control all aspects of your family life or else all hell will break loose! On top of that, she is probably not convinced that you can handle such planning without her (because you handed her the reins of the relationship for so many years). She may have immediately, in her mind, jumped to: *"Let me imagine the twenty-eight ways that he's going to fuck this up."* Plus, if you have been routinely pressuring your wife to have sex with you (the dreaded "Talk"), then she probably views this as yet another ploy to get into her pants.

What you do is simple: You plan everything out. You don't let her words bother you. You don't push for sex. You simply enjoy time away from the kids with your wife. You work on reconnecting as a couple. You allow her to take off her "MOM" uniform and go back to the old, single her… if maybe just for a few days.

Should You Initiate Sex with Your Wife?

One of the most common questions I receive from readers of the first edition of The Dead Bedroom Fix is: *"Wait… I'm confused. Should I initiate with my wife, or not?"*

Context is everything. Your response to your wife is everything. If you've put in the hard work outlined in this book, and you feel the planets are aligned just right, and you're getting signals from your wife that she is open, relaxed, and ready for intimacy, then go ahead and make a move. Be smooth about it. Start slow. Little moves. Back away. More moves. Back away. Make it fun. Make it playful. Don't make it a chore. Don't go full-blown porno star right outta the gate. If she hesitates or acts like she's not ready, back off. No big deal. You're an adult male. You're not a slave to your balls. You're intelligent and mature enough to recognize that your wife isn't there yet. You jumped the gun a little bit. No biggy. We've all done it.

This is where many of you with anxiety issues fumble the ball. To be rejected by your spouse, especially after you believe you have put in so much positive work and you feel she has been giving you go-ahead signals all day, will be a huge blow to your ego. You may have a very visceral, physical reaction to the rejection. That's okay, it's totally understandable. Put on your best possible game face.

Reassure her that it is no big deal, then go to another room or on a long walk to compose yourself. It is important that she gets the impression that you are not seriously phased by her not quite being ready for physical intimacy.

You may find that this new "hey-this-is-no-big-deal" attitude is a GIANT TURNON to your wife.

You're not needy. You're a man. James Bond wouldn't jump up and pout and say, *"It's not fair! You've been giving me signals all day! We're supposed to have sex!"*

Be cool. Baby steps. This stuff takes time.

Here is one uncomfortable, politically incorrect truth:

Women are way more pliable than you think.

After my wife left, both neighbors on either side of our house divorced. The wives left their husbands. It's true. No bullshit. Do you think that was a coincidence? Nope. The ladies talked. They compared notes. A little story here and a little story there, and they were convinced that those little annoying things their husbands did over the years weren't so little after all. In fact, they were pretty big and worthy of rethinking this whole marriage thing. The pros outweighed the cons. The women decided they were better off without their men. Hey, it happens!

Yes, it can be that stupid and drastic. These stories are not unique in any way, shape, or form.

This is precisely why you keep your wife away from the newly divorced alcoholic gal from the office. This is why you should have a little alarm going off in your head when your wife goes on a "girls' night out" three weeks in a row and leaves you with the kids.

Not only do friends act as major influencers over a woman's day-to-day behavior, but the woman's romantic partner can morph her into a completely new human being, as well. Ever watch a woman who is smitten with a guy completely and totally change her lifestyle and demeanor to match that of her lover? It happens ALL the time.

Women tend to be higher in agreeableness and empathy. They are far more social than we are. These personality traits lead to more "go-with-the-flow" type of actions and a tendency to look for direction and follow the strongest leader. In general, it makes women the more submissive sex. Here are a few real-world examples of women who have morphed to take on the traits of their new lover:

1. A buttoned-up, fifty-something conservative grandma and marketing VP who was single for twelve years (her husband cheated on her) finally dates a man who pushes her buttons. He is a huge Harley Davidson enthusiast and motorcycle club member. She quickly becomes a leather-clad, tattooed biker chick with fake boobs. She and her biker boyfriend ride their motorcycles all over the country and they couldn't be happier. She bears zero resemblance to the woman from just a year ago.

2. A boring, "low libido" forty-something mom of three with a Ph.D. has an affair, divorces her husband, and turns into a tattooed, bodybuilding swinger who ignores her children. When she's not participating in orgies or lifting weights, she's routinely on social media proclaiming that she is "the happiest" she's ever been. All her family and friends say she is a completely different human being.

3. A boring, thirty-something housewife and mom of two goes back to school to get her degree. She eventually has sex with three young fraternity guys and divorces her husband to be with one of them. She dresses like she's twenty again, gets a nose piercing, colors her hair, and ignores her children. The new boyfriend is unemployed and spends his time smoking pot in his parents' basement. The ex-husband has majority custody of the kids. If asked, she will say her ex-husband lied and "stole" the kids from her.

All three of the above scenarios occurred in my extended circle of friends. No, these women are not crazy, they're human beings in love. Their buttons have been pushed. This is probably a new feeling for them. When they're in love, they will morph and change into whatever form they feel is necessary to keep their new man around. They do so unconsciously. They feel that their new Lover makes them feel better than they ever have felt before and they don't want to lose that. He is, in essence, a drug that they never want to stop using.

The Lover pushed their buttons, and they reacted in a very

predictable, albeit drastic way. The programming is in motion. The woman's hindbrain has determined that the Mr. Lover Man is worthy of her time, attention, and body. If that means taking on a new persona and flushing away her old life, then so be it.

No, I don't live in some crazy, secret world of cheaters and insane women. This is real life. I could give you 1,000 other real-world examples from guys all over the country who I have talked to over the past few years, as well as the hundreds of thousands of stories online.

All stories end with the same phrase: *"This is not my wife."* This is precisely why I contend that it may be possible to reignite the passion in your "low libido" wife. Create the right atmosphere, project the right mentality, push the right buttons… and you're off to the races.

So, that means YOU should be the leader, and she should just come along for the ride.

Set the tone. Be genuine. Push the buttons. She will follow. You're the guy who is going places. You're the one that is interesting, good-looking, and different from all the other husbands out there.

You're the prize. I could fill an auditorium with single women in your area who would LOVE to be with a man like you.

If your wife wants to jump on this awesome train, she better hurry up and do so.

That's the relationship tone I mentioned earlier, where the woman morphed into a different person. She naturally saw this guy who, in her little world, was just so different and awesome that she submitted completely to him. It doesn't mean he is rich and famous, either, just… different. Often, the new Lover's version of "different" is just "low anxiety, highly confident and outgoing." That can be a drastic and welcoming change from a meek and anxious husband who walks on eggshells around his wife.

These women didn't just morph into a new lifestyle, pretend to like it, and force a smile along the way. No, they were eager and happy to submit and go along for the ride. To have a man who has laid out a blueprint for life and fun puts them at ease—one less thing to worry about!

The supreme irony in all this is that all women, if allowed, will default to being the manager of the family unit. She will plan; she will decide. Eventually, she will grow to hate the job. Every year of being the lone planner and decision-maker will build her resentment and push her libido farther down the hole.

If your woman is making plans, you damn well better jump to attention. Don't place your hands behind your head, put your feet up, and say, *"Oh nice. I don't have to worry about this. My wife can handle it."* You should jump right in, give your opinion, and find out where you can help. Gradually, try taking over the management of the task: *"Okay, babe.*

You go do this and this… and I will take care of the other three things.”

I have heard more than one woman say, *“I would just like for once to not have to make all the decisions about everything. One day I'd like to not have to THINK and just let somebody ELSE do it!”* When your wife perpetually leads the family and your relationship, the tone is invariably one of frustration and anger. She will grow tired of playing taskmaster and the man who so easily submits to her rule. She doesn't want to be the leader of the tribe all day every day.

She gets tired of seeing your clothes on the floor, watching your beer belly grow, hearing you whine about the lack of sex in your marriage, seeing you ignore the chores that need to be done (or worse, doing the chores and seeking her approval), and her being the only one to call and arrange for all those important family events.

She wants a man who takes care of things and always looks to improve himself and the family.

She wants an interesting man. She wants a man who is not afraid of saying what he thinks about her or their relationship at any given moment. She wants a man who won't put up with her bullshit.

In short, she wants it all.

She wants to submit to a guy who throws her on the back of

the proverbial motorcycle and says, *"Hold on,"* as he weaves through traffic on his way to adventure and parts unknown.

That guy gets laid.

CHAPTER 5
HOW OTHERS MAY SEE YOUR CHANGES

"That's manipulation. You're being fake."

If you ever find yourself talking about how to be a better man, or more specifically, how to be a better Lover, you will probably hear some semblance of the above phrase.
By bettering yourself physically, getting away from your family to concentrate on yourself, not putting up with your wife's negative behavior, putting up boundaries, and being open with your sexuality… you're being "manipulative"? Seriously?

Here's what people are really saying:

"You're not actually being YOU. We much prefer to see the real YOU, and not some fake guy going through the motions and pretending to be more than what he REALLY is. If you're a true, natural, all-around great dude, then that's great. If you're just a weak guy who is pretending and TRYING to be a good all-around dude, then no…. that's not good. We will openly shame you for that."

Remember, people want to associate with "natural" men, not guys who are learning how to be better and more attractive. Of course, the concept of the "natural" is ridiculous. Nobody was born with an innate knowledge of how to be attractive and get laid. They learned over the years by watching others. Some guys just make it look way too easy. Trust me, these "natural" Lover guys had many drinks thrown in their faces and have enough embarrassing memories to last a lifetime.

Look at who is doing the shaming. Look at who is most vocally against your "manipulative" behavior:

1. **Women:** These are the same women who put on makeup, color their hair, lie about their age, wear spandex leggings to hide their cellulite, and lie about the number of men they have slept with.

These same women are concerned about men being "manipulative"? Seriously? Of course. This is their game, not yours.

To be disingenuous in the mating game is accepted as being in the woman's realm, not the man's. The man must present his TRUE self so that the woman doesn't make the giant mistake of picking the wrong guy. Remember, it's a huge deal for a woman to pick a man. There's a lot riding on her decision (babies, resources, etc.). She can't put up with any bullshit.

The "no manipulation" rule does not apply to her. Manipulation is an essential element of the female dating game. It's up to men to figure out what is real and what isn't. The more in the dark men are, the better.

Men playing the same manipulation game is just plain creepy.

2. **Weak men:** There is an understood dominance hierarchy among men. Get a group of guys together and somebody will invariably come out as the leader. The

rest will fall behind. Picture it as a pyramid of power. The powerful are the few at the tippy top of the pyramid, with most of the rest at the wide base at the bottom.

The same applies to the world of relationships. When a man at the bottom of the pyramid watches as the few men at the top get all the sex, he will grow resentful. He still has his overwhelming urge to have sex with as many women as possible, so he does what he can to elbow his way into the top-tier group and stake his claim. That may mean trying to sabotage the efforts of the higher-ranking men (cock-blocking, in other words). That may also mean befriending women with the sneaky purpose of getting sex somewhere down the line (trying to escape the friend zone).

These men are the true creeps. They are conniving and manipulative to the core. Some of you reading this may be realizing that YOU were once one of these guys.

These men are some of the first to put down your efforts towards self-improvement. Be aware of them, but they should be ignored completely. Their loser mentality is infectious. Remember, their worries never come from a place of true empathy, but rather from a place of competition. They are attempting to sabotage your efforts as a man trying to rise in the hierarchy.

People often put men and women into comfortable categories and roles: *"You… you're a Provider. You… you're a mom. You… you're a slut."* When you go outside of those little boxes they put you in, people react almost with hostility and disbelief.

This is especially true if you are encroaching on their territory.

Watch the needy but sweet guy walk up to the pretty girl at the bar and tell her that she has a great body, or worse… try to touch her. Watch the scantily clad "slutty" girl interview for a position at a daycare center.

The reaction is always the same, some variation of: *"Uhhh… what are YOU doing HERE? Aren't you supposed to be somewhere ELSE? Get outta here!"*

You may receive the same type of hostile disbelief or anger when you attempt to shed some of your Provider/Pushover/Nice Guy behaviors in the hopes of earning more Lover points and rewards. You've been playing the same role for YEARS now. People won't know what the hell to think about your radical behavior change. Some will flat-out hate you for it.

This is very troubling to a lot of men. *"I'm still the same sweet guy!"* they say to their partner and old friends… only to be hated even more. Why? Because you failed their shit test. They actually RESPECTED the new you more than the old you. They poked at you a little to see if the changes were genuine. You folded. Now they know you belong to the group of weak and manipulative men that everyone detests. Remember that you're trying to better yourself and, consequently, improve your marriage with your wife. You're doing nothing wrong. Stay the course. You're making positive progress. Every person who has experienced a modicum of success will tell you that the phenomenon of people trying to test you and throw you off your mission is VERY common. We call this the "crabs-in-the-bucket" phenomenon. You try to crawl your way out, and your buddy, family member, colleague, or spouse tries to PULL you back down to their level.

It's a perfectly natural and expected reaction to your hard work and changes. It's heartbreaking to see people you love turn on you so quickly. We all believe that our spouses will be our biggest cheerleaders, so to see the exact opposite is shocking to us.

Eventually, if you do your job right, they will gladly come along for the ride. If they don't, you leave them behind forever.

CHAPTER 6
HOLY SHIT, IT WORKED

"Work hard in silence. Let success make the noise."

—Anonymous

Your "Eureka!" Moment Has Arrived

It took months of difficult changes on your part… but you finally did it.

You come home one day, and there is a text from your wife as soon as you walk in the door. It simply says, *"Go to the bedroom."* You head toward the bedroom expecting some major disaster requiring your attention. Maybe there is a wasp in the closet again, or the dog took a giant shit on the carpet. You walk down the hall, turn the corner and you're shocked to find your wife, naked, covered in baby oil, lying on the bed saying, *"It's about time you got home."*

Holy shit, it worked. You pushed the right buttons in the right combination and her sexual engine fired up again.

You did it.

But wait… there's a rub. There's always a rub. You thought it was going to be that easy?

You may not want her anymore.

"Wait, what?! There's no way!" you're saying right now. Yep. This is common. This is the "bad" part of going through major life changes and dramatic self-improvement. This is the bad part of overcoming your anxious persona and embodying a confidence you've never had before.

YOU FINALLY RECOGNIZE YOUR WORTH.

This is precisely why your wife was so nervous about your sudden change in behavior. What she knew deep down was true: She may not be able to match your new level of self-improvement. Your vast improvements in physical appearance, confidence, and overall attitude have also fully exposed her faults as a romantic partner.

Let's be honest, your wife is no spring chicken anymore. She knows that it is not uncommon for older attractive men to have a girlfriend half their age. She knows she cannot compete with Buffy the hot little twenty-two-year-old at the gym who all the guys drool over.

No amount of makeup, boob jobs, or time at the gym can turn back the hands of time and allow her to compare favorably to Bimbo Buffy at the most primal and shallow level of "attraction." She's fully aware of this fact. She's seen the porn videos that you were caught looking at. She's seen you unconsciously staring at girls in public. She knows what all these women have in common. She knows what pushes your buttons.

She also can't magically erase the years of resentment you have built up after going so long without sexual intimacy. She is one nervous and anxious spouse right now, and for good reason.

You're pissed. You're horny. You're a high-value man in a sea of attractive single women. You've been hit on or approached by a few of these ladies over the past few months. Bimbo Buffy at the gym actually said hi and smiled at you the other day. This has never happened to you before. It's exhilarating. These women are pushing your caveman buttons, big time.

If you're being totally honest, these women make your wife look very blah and unattractive. You feel terrible for thinking this way, but there's no way around it. They're hot. Your wife is not. Your wife gave up on trying to win your admiration and affection long ago.

Your dramatic self-improvements have opened a new world for you, a new circle of friends. You're now around people who also take self-improvement to heart. New guy friends. New female admirers. Consequently, your admiration and attraction for your wife has dwindled. Coming home to her just doesn't have the same appeal that it used to. Being around your wife is a major downer.

"Lucky" for you, your wife finally woke up and said, *"Alright… I see all these improvements you've made, Mr. Husband. Now I'm genuinely turned on and I will gladly allow you access to my body. Please come to the bedroom for your reward."*

You had to jump through A LOT of hoops to get to this point. Really tough stuff. Life-altering self-improvement. Sacrifices. She simply had to sit there and flip a switch in her head, get turned on, and finally realize what a great all-around guy she is married to.

It's at this point you may get a great deal of satisfaction by looking at her on the bed and saying to her, *"Not tonight, honey. I have a headache,"* as you walk away and pump your fist like you just hit a home run in the World Series.

Don't be petty. Don't be a vindictive little bitch. Be a man. Life presents you with a lot of tests and temptations, and this is one of them. My advice is to be the leader. Show her how things are done. Set aside your ego. This is your time to shine.

Bang the living snot out of that woman.

Take all those frustrations out in the bedroom. Your attitude should be, *"Here, let me show you what you've been missing."* Make sure for the rest of the week she has a big goofy smile on her face and a pronounced limp.

You made vows; you stick to them. You're a man. That's what you do. If all of us jumped ship every time the grass looked greener elsewhere, there would be no stability in life. The family structure would dissolve. We would all be a bunch of selfish assholes jumping from person to person until we turn eighty and realize that we should've just worked harder on our relationships, instead of throwing our hands up and walking away when things got tough.

The grass is not greener on the other side. The grass is greener where you water it.

Use your new level of attractiveness, energy, and self-worth as a guide for your wife's future behavior. The new theme is, *"This is the way things are going to be from now on."* You're going to lead. You're going to be awesome and attractive, and she is going to appreciate it and reciprocate.

She's going to put the same effort into her own self-improvement and work on your marriage.

You're worth it and she's worth it.

The results will be sexy, fun, and positive. Yes, it's going to be tough. Really tough. This is why they say, *"Relationships are hard work."*

Again, that doesn't mean you are telling her, *"Fuck me, or I leave, woman!"* This means you are now acutely aware of what a dead bedroom signifies. It means the relationship is on its last legs.

You've done all YOU can to remedy the situation, now it's up to her to do the same. It takes two to tango. She can choose to jump on board the "healthy relationship" train, or not. Up to her. But, she needs to know that the ride won't be an easy one. To keep up with such an awesome husband has its rewards, and its downsides.

About "Pity Sex"

After publishing the first edition of The Dead Bedroom Fix, some of the most commonly asked questions I received from readers revolved around the topic of "pity sex." "Pity sex" is what we call the sex that our wives offer us even though they are obviously not turned on. They do so out of obligation… or just to shut us up. Anyone who has a sense of empathy and a smidgen of social awareness can spot "pity sex" a mile away.

Often, when a guy starts his journey of self-improvement, his wife will pick up on it right away.

First, it starts as: *"Hmmm… something is weird here."* She will poke and prod and look for something insidious bubbling under the surface. When she fails at uncovering anything sinister, she's left with the realization: *"Oh, he's just getting better. He's getting more attractive. Now I'm kinda scared I may lose him and my entire comfortable existence may come to an end."* While this may be the beginning of the process of genuine attraction and appreciation, it's not the entire recipe you need to make the complete *"wife-is-crazy-about-me"* stew you're looking for.

Your wife: *"We can have sex tonight if you want."* This can happen relatively quickly. After all, thanks to *"women's intuition"* she can pick up on changes in social dynamics fairly easily. She knows something is up, she knows it can lead to something really "wrong," so she does what she feels is the foolproof method for getting her husband back in line: She offers him sex.

My word of advice is this: You don't have to have sex if you don't want to. If your eyes and your gut are telling you, *"This doesn't feel right,"* and you're sure that she's offering you sex for the wrong reasons, then politely decline. I think you should err on the side of complete honesty:

> *"Honey, you don't have to do that. I realize you FEEL like you have to, but you don't. Really. Your body language is all off. You don't look the least bit into it. I'd much prefer to wait until you're 100% comfortable and really in the mood. Okay? Honestly… no hard feelings at all. I get it completely. I love you, beautiful."*

Wow, your wife won't know what to think. She will be further anxious, concerned, confused… and she will respect the hell out of you. Why? Because you're a man who is not a slave to his balls. You're not some horny teen who grabs at the first opportunity for sex and uses his wife like a sex doll. You're a man who has the social intelligence and the heart to say, *"I see what's going on here… it's not good. No thank you."*

Some women may get flustered and seemingly angry about this new plot twist: *"Well, if you're going to wait until I'm really into it, then don't hold your breath. It's not going to happen."*

Ouch. Not a very nice thing to say. Just smile back and say, "Okay." Continue doing your thing. Or, get a little frisky back at her: "*Well, then… yer gonna miss out. I'm pretty hot.*"

Smack her butt as you walk away.

Now you're REALLY going to see a confused wife!

I know what you want. We all want it. You want true passion and desire. Your wife does, too. Be the leader and show her what is acceptable and what isn't. Show her that you don't have to settle for scraps. You can wait until you have the full recipe and the delicious sex stew you so rightly deserve.

Don't Get Comfortable

Trust me, it will take NO time at all to wipe out all the hard work you put into making all these positive changes. At times, it will seem like the whole world is conspiring to bring you down and squash all your positive results. There will be temptations around every corner: awesome food to eat, lazy Sundays with a stack of pancakes and a couch calling your name, friends making fun of you for working out so much, family worried that you seem to have lost so much weight. "Are you ill? You're not eating enough!"

What will astound you is that your WIFE will seem to be the one who's most eager to sabotage your efforts. That's right, the one person who benefits the most from your changes (other than yourself) will try her damnedest to bring you down.

You think you've seen "tests" before? Well, just wait. You ain't seen nothing yet, amigo.

You're going to present to her a new man who pushes her buttons and makes her sexual engine rev back up. This is huge. This is no minor occurrence. This throws everything off balance. Her hindbrain is going to be screaming, "THIS IS AMAZING… BUT MAKE SURE HE IS FOR REAL!"

You'll get little insults at strange times. You'll get complaints. She'll try to shame you out of going to the gym. She'll question why you're dressing so nicely. She'll get more jealous. She'll start getting angry again about you looking at that woman at the mall for a split second. She may even attempt to shame you for it.

You shouldn't care one little bit.

This is the time when a lot of guys fold… and then they have to start all over again. *"Well, I mean.. she IS giving me sex now, so maybe I should ease up a bit."*

Don't you dare change. You'll be back to your old life faster than you can say Pornhub.com.

Remember, watch what she does, not what she says.

Look at your wife's appearance. I'll bet it has improved; sex has gone up. When she's not throwing random tests your way, she's brighter and more energetic. Her spark has returned.

Married life is better overall.

Recognize the intent and feeling behind these random tests from your wife is fear, not anger. It's insecurity. She's scared of losing you and she's also scared that she's letting her guard down for a man that is not genuine. She's afraid that she's trusting a fraud. Show her comfort by continuing to be the best man you can be. Show her love and appreciation. Continue to improve. Don't put up with her bullshit… and bang her with the force of a thousand rabid hyenas.

Remember, with sex comes drama. With drama comes sex.

It's all part of the game.

CHAPTER 7
IT DIDN'T WORK

"Failure is only the opportunity to begin again, and this time more wisely."

—Henry Ford

I'm not going to bullshit you. All your hard work may not result in sex from your wife.

Yes, that's right. You could very well become the absolute best version of yourself, stop doing the Five Mistakes, stop putting up with your wife's bullshit, be a more loving partner, be a great leader… and she may still have no interest in sex or any kind of intimacy with you.

So, what's going on here?

Well, it could be a variety of things. It could be something terrible, like she is seeing somebody else on the side and wrote you off long ago. It could be that she has a great deal of resentment towards you (possibly for very valid reasons). She may view all these improvements and changes as happening way too late in the game. It could be hormonal. Is she menopausal? Hormones can have a dramatic effect on a person's sex drive. For many women, menopause means that they close the chapter on their sexuality for good.

It could be that she never really was into you sexually but viewed you only as a provider of resources she needed for her and her future children. That's not unheard of.

Many times, a man at this stage in the game becomes clear-headed and has a great number of epiphanies about his marriage. The fog of his previous Provider-centric role has lifted, and he now sees things from a more "complete" and healthier viewpoint. What was once a woman who he raised children and maintained a home with is now a very angry and cold person who hasn't shown him affection for years.

The Anxious/Avoidant Dynamic

Let's pause for a moment here and talk about a dynamic that I see all too often with my coaching clients and members of our HFM Brotherhood group (learn more at helpformen. com/join).

Many, dare I say MOST of you guys who are reading this, are what we call "anxious" individuals, and you exhibit what psychologists call "anxious attachment." You may also hear it referred to as "preoccupied attachment." You can read more on the topic here: helpformen.com/articles/a-guys-guide-attachment-styles

In short, you are the anxious pursuer in the relationship. You are preoccupied with the state of the relationship. You are often referred to as the clingy or needy person of the two. You crave intimacy and connection, but you fear being rejected or abandoned. You tend to overthink things and catastrophize situations within the relationship. You're the one who is suggesting that your partner reads certain books, listens to podcasts, watches videos, and goes to marriage counseling.

You can be a real handful to a person whose nature isn't so anxious.

Unfortunately for you guys, you tend to match up with the polar opposite of the anxious attachment person: the avoidant.

Ironic, isn't it? You dated, married, and had kids with the person who is the exact opposite of what your temperament needs.

As the name implies, the avoidant AVOIDS any real intimacy. Once they are past the drunken honeymoon stage of the relationship, they just shut down. They value their independence and self-sufficiency above everything else in their life. They view your clingy and needy ways as a real threat to their freedom and autonomy. If this sounds like kind of a "masculine" mindset, that's for good reason. Most avoidants tend to be men. But, as I've learned over the years, there are A LOT of avoidant women out there, and their husbands tend to find my material.

Where do these anxious and avoidant attachment styles come from? Like everything else in this relationship game, they can be traced back to childhood. So many men I have talked to have told me that their wives grew up in a household with little to no physical affection. Mom and Dad didn't kiss. They didn't hug. When Dad walked in the door after work, nobody jumped up to ask him about his day. The wife grew up in an extremely cold environment. Their mom was probably the boss of the family, and the dad was probably the meek little guy who just kept quiet and spent time in his workshop.

Does this sound familiar? Does this describe your wife's family? If so, your wife had a front-row seat for how exactly

NOT to maintain a healthy and loving relationship. That programming has been ingrained in her for decades. She quite literally does not see the benefit of being close and intimate with her partner. In fact, it's probably a huge turnoff to her.

You, my friend, are probably not going to be able to fix that particular situation with advice from one little book. If you want your wife to change and morph into the type of person that is appealing to your more anxious temperament, then you're asking her to fundamentally change aspects of her personality. I'm sorry to say that it's probably not going to happen. If it does, it will take YEARS of intense therapy… which begins with her raising her hand and saying, *"I need help."*

You know your wife better than anyone. How likely is that to happen?

On the flip side, YOU need to work on your anxious form of attachment. That is precisely what is outlined in this book. When you get far enough along your journey of self-improvement, you are hopefully stripping away some of the anxieties and self-loathing that contribute to your anxious form of attachment. That's why your partner may not be so attractive to you anymore. You're no longer anxious. Therefore, you're now looking at your avoidant partner through the eyes of a more secure individual.

Secure men don't like avoidant women. They run away from them.

Admittedly, these avoidant partner situations exist on a spectrum. Some women are a little avoidant, and some are extremely so. If your wife is an eleven on a scale from one to ten, then you should probably give strong consideration to moving on without her. Your mental health will thank you.

When Your Work Doesn't Pay Off

"My wife has said, in no uncertain terms, that she wants nothing to do with me... but she continues to stick around. Why?"

Wives who are "over" their relationships typically don't just walk up to their husbands and say, "We're done" (unless another man is in the picture). Instead, they will gradually plant seeds of disdain in the hopes that their man will take the not-so-subtle hints and get the ball rolling himself. This allows the women to save face and play victim, but still get out of the awful, life-sucking relationship.

Win/Win for her.

What she doesn't know is that her man is so conditioned and so broken (anxious) that he will just double down on his "positive" attributes (the Five Mistakes) and hope to turn things around. He's dug in like a tick, and it's going to take a lot to shake him free.

Men use their sense of "honor" as a badge of courage when it's really just an excuse to roll over, expose their belly, and submit to a wife who is nothing short of disgusted by them.

Another word for this "honor" that men cling to is "codependency," which is another name for "relationship addiction." You need them, and you need them to need you. A codependent person often puts their partner's needs before their own. A codependent person often takes on the role of the martyr. (Many of you saw this growing up with a codependent parent.) They see all the terrible things their partner does, and they brush it under the rug. Oftentimes, they cover up and protect their abusive or unhealthy partner's behavior. The codependent sees themselves as a victim, and they tend to befriend and form romantic relationships with others that allow them to act out this martyr/rescuer persona.

This is not a path towards a mentally healthy life. It can have horrible consequences.

I've heard horror stories from men about wives who treat them with over-the-top disdain. One man caught his wife spitting into his drink when she thought he wasn't looking. Another found text messages from his wife to another man saying that she hoped her husband's cancer treatment wouldn't work so that he could hurry up and die. Another man watched his wife make fun of his asthma to a group of friends… rolling her eyes in disgust.

Women are human beings. They are capable of some pretty malevolent behavior. If they feel that they are pushed into a corner (like being trapped in a boring life with a man they have lost respect for), they will act out. They may build up resentment and no-holds-barred hatred for their husband

and act accordingly.

So, why doesn't YOUR wife respond positively to any of your positive life changes?

Who knows? Who cares?

You are only responsible for you. You are not responsible for the opinions and actions of others. Sometimes that is disappointing and incredibly heartbreaking. It can also be extremely liberating.

You get to be what YOU want to be. That is life in a nutshell. Always remember one thing: Relationships, by their nature, are very difficult. Anyone who tells you otherwise is either bullshitting you, somehow lucked into a perfect partnership, or they are just "naturals" at navigating the turbulent relationship waters.

They may be one of the chosen few who make this whole game look easy. They probably grew up in an amazing household with amazing parents and an amazing extended family of grandparents, aunts, uncles, cousins, and siblings. They all probably have great relationships with their spouses. Everyone is sitting back and watching each other succeed. They're learning from each other.

If you're reading this book, that's probably not your family story… and probably not your wife's story, either.

Marriage takes a certain disposition, a certain personality, and a specific set of life and relationship skills that most of us just flat-out do not have.

If you stop and look at the modern-day interpretation of marriage, it's damn near impossible to get it right. Those of us wanting to get married are saying:

- ✓ I want to be married to my best friend.

- ✓ I want to be married to a good earner. Going through life is tough. We need money. We need security.

- ✓ I want to be married to somebody I admire. No respect means I don't stick around.

- ✓ I want to be married to my lover. I want to have desire for them consistently, and vice-versa.

- ✓ I want to be married to my caregiver. I may get ill or incapacitated, and I want my spouse to be there for me no matter what.

Basically, we're saying, *"I want to have all of my relationship needs put into one human being from now until the day I die. I want my friend, my parent, and my sexual lover all wrapped into one person."*

Wow… that's a lot of pressure. That's quite the list of expectations.

No wonder it fails so often!

But man… when it works… it's a beautiful thing.

Is it worth all of your hard work? Are you up for the challenge?

Well, unfortunately, you're just one half of the equation. She has to want it, too… and she may very well not see the need or have any desire to improve upon your current marital situation, no matter what you do.

It sucks, but it's extremely common. Your wife gave up on your marriage. She's content with the status quo. She likes the mediocrity because it serves her needs just fine.

Don't feel too bad about yourself. This is not the time for a pity party. You're desirable. The new you could get laid next week by a pretty woman who just wants to have fun with a guy exactly like you. Your wife still saying, "Get away from me," should NOT be a giant, reality-shattering event. It's just a fork in the road of life. It's tough… but not unexpected and by no means life-ending. In fact, the fun has just begun, as you will quickly learn.

A good life lesson for you is not to gauge your worth based on the fickle opinions of others. You've done too much hard work and too many good things up to this point to say, *"If she doesn't like me, then there must still be something wrong with me."*

Maybe there is. Maybe there isn't.

Who gives a shit?

You should be content with the fact that you did absolutely EVERYTHING you could have done to save your marriage. You presented the absolute best "husband" package possible to your wife. You accepted the challenge that comes with being a married man and faced it head-on. You worked hard. You did everything by the book.

1. You're objectively more attractive.
2. You're healthier.
3. You have more energy.
4. You have stronger boundaries and more confidence.
5. Other women find you attractive.
6. Men look up to you.
7. You've made your attraction to your wife and intent known.
8. You're a loving and attentive husband.

All these positive things occurred in your life as a result of your hard work, and yet your wife says, *"Meh… I don't think so."*

Well, that's her problem.

You're a damn good husband. You're a good man; don't forget that. With or without your wife, you are still YOU.

The dead bedroom signifies that there are major issues with

your relationship. You just tried all you could to reignite your love life. You have been rejected. Your romantic relationship is over.

It's time to leave your wife.

Surprised I would suggest ending the marriage? Remember what I said at the beginning of this book: *"This book was written for heterosexual men in long-term monogamous relationships who want more sex."*

I didn't say, *"More sex from your wife."*

You're a good-looking, confident, interesting, fit, manly, kind, and hard-working dude.

I promise you. You'll be more than fine.

CHAPTER 8
FREQUENTLY ASKED QUESTIONS & COMMENTS

Ever since I wrote the first edition of The Dead Bedroom Fix, I have received A LOT of emails from readers. Here are a few of the most common ones:

1. *"I want to get away from the house more. You said in the book that the Lover doesn't really tell the woman his whereabouts or what he is doing. I tried this and my wife flipped out and said it was not a good thing. She didn't know if I was alive or dead."*

Well… the quintessential Lover also dates and has sex with several different women at once. I don't suggest that for a married man… much like I don't suggest you run off and not tell the wife where you're going. I wouldn't expect my wife to do that, either. It would be weird.

When you're a married man with kids, it's important that you strike a balance between Lover and Provider. In my opinion, just walking out the door of your house and not telling anyone where you are going is strange. There's nothing wrong with saying, *"Heading out to get some things done. Be back in a couple of hours. I may hit the gym, too. I'll let you know."* You're not just dating the woman casually; you're her husband and father to her children.

2. *"Should I tell my wife about this book? She's already noticed my change in behavior and is suspicious."*

In other words, you're scared that your wife may think you're up to no good. You want to alleviate her anxiety. You want to prove to her that your actions are done in a positive way. No, don't tell her. Stay the course. You're doing nothing wrong. I repeat, you're doing nothing wrong. Stop looking for mommy's permission and stop trying to fix her perceived negative emotions over something silly like, *"my husband is finally acting like a man, so something must be wrong."*

3. *"My wife says I've been nothing but a huge asshole since I read The Dead Bedroom Fix. Our sex life hasn't improved at all. The other day I was going out the door and she asked me where I was going. I just said, 'Out.' She blew up my phone with angry text messages. I ignored her. She later asked me if there was something I was pissed about. I wanted to tell her, 'Yes. I'm pissed that we haven't had sex since our two-year-old was born,' but I know that's exactly what I shouldn't do. We've had those talks fifty times already. It doesn't do anything. Not sure what to do. I just told her that no, nothing is wrong."*

I think your simply saying, "Out," came across as pissy and angry. And rightfully so. You're pissy and angry. SHE KNOWS exactly what you're upset about (at least, in part). How do I know she knows? Because you're a man and you've had the dreaded talk fifty times already. It has obviously affected you a great deal, and you're letting her know that in a very passive-aggressive way. Either get over it, move on and try to better yourself (regardless of her feelings), or simply tell her that you're not happy with the way the relationship is going, you're trying to process things, and you wish to be alone instead of whining to her like you always do.

4. *"So, I read your book and was ready to start putting in the hard work to become a better man, but my wife surprised me by asking if I've ever thought about having an open marriage. That was a shock, to say the least. What do you think about open marriages? Good idea? Seems to be a good solution to our situation."*

I think your wife is cheating on you. Allow me to explain...

For a woman to ask a man if he would consider being okay with her having intercourse with other men while remaining in the marriage (the definition of an "open marriage")... that takes some real confidence and nerve to bring up.

First, it may be that your relationship is pretty open and sexual in that way, always has been, and the "open marriage" idea feels like a natural progression in your relationship timeline. Perhaps it's something you have done with partners in the past. Considering that you are reading this book, I'm going to go out on a limb and say that does NOT apply to you.

Second, it may be that your wife doesn't feel any danger in bringing the topic up with you because she has no fear of your negative response. Most men hearing such a thing from their wives, especially if they are in a long-term dead bedroom situation, would react VERY negatively. Your wife is not stupid and knows this, so why bring it up so flippantly? Because... she has a safety net. That safety net is the presence of another romantic partner. If you say yes, she gets to keep the comfort and stability of your relationship and carry on in a new, sexy relationship with her lover... and it's all above board! She's not a bad person! If you say no, she learns that she will need to hide her affair from you and/or divorce you to be with him. That's a messy situation, but it's one that I see happening more often than not. Woman connects with new man, forms bond, leaves old partner. Pretty simple stuff.

5. *"My problem is that your book assumes that there was a super sexual point early in the relationship. My relationship with my wife has never been sexual. I've always felt like a pervert for wanting to do sexy things with her. She hates doing anything beyond missionary in the dark... and I get that maybe once a month if I'm lucky. After our child was born, we went a year and a half without sex. Not all relationships can be saved, I'm afraid."*

You're absolutely right. Read Chapter 7 again.

6. *"I loved the book and I agree with everything you said, but I really don't think this will work with my wife. We're so far gone it's not even funny. I'm afraid I've started an emotional affair with another woman and I'm to the point where I don't even care if my wife finds out. What did she expect? Am I wrong for having these needs?"*

No, you're not wrong for having needs. You're not wrong for lusting after another woman. You're wrong for not doing the adult thing and sitting down with your wife and telling her it's over. Instead, you're taking the chickenshit way out and fooling around with another woman. You don't want to disrupt the comfort and stability of home life, but you also want to have your kicks on the side. You wouldn't be the first man in history to have an affair, and you also won't be the first to have his life blow up when his wife finds out (and she will find out).

7. *"I read The Dead Bedroom Fix, but I was disappointed. It was basically all about going to the gym. There's more to being a man than just muscles. Not all of us want to be meatheads."*

I can't tell you how many times I've been told this; it always baffles me. The gym is literally step one of a multi-step process outlined in the book. Why do so many men stop there and shut the book in disgust? Well, they're looking into a giant mirror and their glaring faults are staring right back at them. Nobody likes being told, *"You have a glaring negative trait and it's all your fault."* Nobody likes being told, *"You have a lot of work to do and that may involve doing physical things that are BELOW your perceived value."*

Many Ph.D. and higher education types bristle at the thought of their brainy wives being turned on by muscles. Many of these guys also learn the hard way that their multiple degrees and their splendid doctoral dissertations don't make their wives' panties fly off. Then, they get really upset when they catch her with the pool man who can barely string together a coherent thought.
The book is not all about the gym. Don't be ridiculous. You just got scared when you read the truth and you threw the book down in disgust.

8. *"My marriage started falling apart due to money issues. I lost my job early on and had a really hard time finding another one. We had to live off of my wife's income for over a year. Now I'm back to making more than what I did before, but we're still paying off debt. Our sex life went into the toilet as soon as I lost my job, and it hasn't been back since. I don't think getting in shape and being more assertive will help my situation. I think my problem is a common one and I'm surprised it wasn't covered in the book."*

Your marriage broke down because your wife's security was threatened. You could've accomplished the same thing by having an affair, a secret drug habit, or something else that says to your wife, "Sorry, you didn't pick the right guy." Instead, you lost your job and didn't get a new one right away. You put her in the role of the breadwinner. No, that's not a good formula for marital happiness. Yes, money is a huge stressor for anyone… but I can't tell you how many men tell me a story very similar to yours… only to discover that his wife was having a torrid affair with some unemployed loser.

Just food for thought.

9. *"I'm confused about the concept of 'shit tests.' I find that my wife is constantly making disrespectful remarks. I've been good about ignoring them, but yesterday she told me that she can tell I'm pissed off and wants to know why."*

There's a fine line between "typical wife shit test behavior" and "toxic disrespectful behavior that needs to be called out immediately." Context is everything.

If you're on your way to the gym and your wife says, *"Do you HAVE to go? Couldn't you stay here instead? You're always going to the gym. I was hoping we could stay in and snuggle today,"* that is a shit test. She's seeing how committed you are to your mission. She wants to see what you're made of. This should not piss you off. This should show you that you're on the right path and that she loves you.

If your wife says, *"I don't know why you are going to the gym. You still look the same as you always have. I don't know who you're trying to impress. It's not like you're ever going to look good with your shirt off,"* she's being disrespectful. Of course this upsets you.

Here's a phrase I try to teach a man to use when his wife is disrespectful and toxic:

"Okay, why would you say that? I can't imagine ever talking to you that way. It's extremely disrespectful and I expect a lot better from you. Do you understand me?"

That's not needy. That's not feminine. That's not weak. That's being a strong guy who's not afraid to call out bad behavior when it happens. He can deal with the subsequent drama.

10. *"My wife literally told me on our honeymoon that she's glad we don't have to have sex so often anymore. It's been ten years, and I should've taken her more seriously. We rarely have sex and it's only during ovulation time. We only have sex*

for the purpose of having kids. She openly admits this. Do you think there is any hope for me to turn this around?"

Nope. Run.

The honeymoon phase of the relationship is supposed to be hypersexual. Yes, even after marriage (in the relationship talk sphere, the "honeymoon phase" refers to the early part of the relationship, regardless of marital status). When somebody literally ANNOUNCES to you that they will stop being so sexual just because of a formal wedding ceremony, that is a pretty blunt indicator of what is to come. They are, I'm sorry to say, a broken individual and you are most definitely not on the same page when it comes to intimacy. A more secure person would've heard that from their new bride, and then quickly gone to an attorney for an annulment.

The typical timeline of a relationship consists of a very hypersexual early phase, followed by a gradual decline in sexual frequency when typical life things get in the way (age, kids, bills, work, etc.). To hear so early on from your partner that they have unilaterally decided to suddenly shut off the sexual intimacy... is very troubling. There are, most likely, very big things going on beneath the surface with your spouse. It's not your job to fix her. If you both decide to work on this relationship, you need to prepare yourself for years of therapy to get to a baseline level of "normal," and from what I have seen over the years... your newfound confidence and years of resentment will take your patience down to near zero.

You also need therapy to work on yourself and try to figure out WHY you condoned such behavior for so long.
I recommend you do so outside of the confines of this relationship. Move on, brother.

11. *"My wife says that her friends all admit to not having sex much at all. None of her friends give their husbands oral sex. She says this is normal and it's very unfair of me to expect more than our typical once-per-month session. Is she right?"*

What do YOU want? Why do you care what her friends say? I would literally laugh if my wife said that to me. You're a healthy adult male. If what she says is true, those husbands are living in hell. You don't want to stay there with them, do you?

CHAPTER 9
READER STORIES

I thought I would share some of the stories from readers of the first edition of The Dead Bedroom Fix. Do you have your own story to share? Please feel free to shoot me a message at ralph.b@helpformen.com. I try my best to read and reply to every email.

(Note: Before we started the Help For Men organization, I used to be known under the pen name "DSO", which stood for "Dad Starting Over.")

"DSO,

Okay, this book was so much like my story that I thought you were spying on me. One thing that stuck out to me was the part where you talk about men discovering that their asexual wife was really slutty in her past. That was totally my story. After we had our kid, my wife shut down sex completely. At first, we could only use hands on each other (still sore from the baby)… then we could just cuddle and make out… then we could only cuddle… then we could only hold hands. After I literally cried to her about our lack of sex (wow I was such a pussy), she told me that she thought she may be asexual. She said she literally had no more sex drive, and she never really did. She said sex was never really important to her. I asked her if that meant she was faking it all the first couple of years of our relationship because she seemed to enjoy it quite a bit back then. She said that yes, she thought she was. She wasn't sure. That always confused me. How do you not know if you enjoyed sex?? Seems to be a pretty cut-and-dried thing to me. Something in my gut said that my wife's comment about being asexual was really weird and wrong. I knew she was sexual before. I knew she had relationships before me. I remembered you saying something about women cheating is common, so I started spying on her (not my proudest moment). I didn't find an affair, but I did find a conversation with one of her friends that made my jaw drop. She admitted to her friend that she was really 'experimental' when she was in her 20s and had two different threesomes. She said she loved every minute of it. She told her friend all the dirty details. It was like reading porn. Then she said the thing that really hit me: 'I forget what it's like to be wanted and sexy. I don't feel like a woman anymore.' WOW. No mention of me at all. Her friend didn't even ask. It was like I didn't exist. I was begging her for sex for YEARS. I was crushed. That was my lowest point. Like your book said, my wife wanted sex but just not with me.

I saw your book on my Instagram feed. I bought it and read it all on the same day. It hit me so hard that I vowed right then and there to change myself completely. If my 'asexual' wife didn't want me, then so be it. I'm only thirty-eight, so I'm literally in the prime of my life. I couldn't go on living like that. I was looking forward to my new life without her. I lost thirty pounds in four months. I changed my wardrobe completely. I started being more of a leader at the office and at home. I stopped asking for sex. I was still loving and sweet when my wife deserved it, but I never took it to the next level and asked her for sex. Never. I could tell that my wife was really confused. It was around month number three that she started to act flirty and sexy around me. That's when she started asking me if I was happy with us. I just told her that there was always room for improvement. I tried to avoid the conversation. I just kept busy and went out of the house. I would spend a lot of time at my friend's house helping him put together a new wood shop in his basement. We would drink beers and talk while working. It was great. When I wasn't with my friend I was at the gym. When I was home I would do my part and help clean up and take care of the kids. I never made a move towards my wife. Ever.

About a month after our talk my wife texted me a link to a video on Pornhub. She asked me if we could please do the things in the video. I had to pick my jaw up off the floor. I thought it was a joke or a test at first. I was actually kind of mad. I wanted to text her back: 'What happened to you being ASEXUAL?!' I didn't reply right away. I decided to take things in the other direction. I played the dominant role and told her that I expected her to be completely nude and bent over for me in bed when I got home. And guess what… she was! Of all our years together, that was the absolute best sex we've ever had.

My wife tests me all the damn time now. I usually pass the tests. That's probably my least favorite part of this change: constant testing. But she's never been happier. We have sex at least three times a week now. What's funny is that now our sex is very dom/sub where I tell her what to do, she follows, and we use all kinds of toys. We even take the dom/sub arrangement outside of the bedroom. It's something that we've both really gotten into and learned a lot about. It's amazing.

Thanks so much for writing the book. You've literally saved my marriage and given me the best sex life I could imagine. R."

"DSO,

Just wanted to send an email to say thanks for putting together some help for guys going through the rough times in their marriage.
I've taken what you've said on board and it's helped more than any counseling sessions I've been to.
As a result, my wife and I are more intimate and more playful, which is really what my goal was. I find the difficult part now is not sliding back into the same mindset as before (which is where I screwed up) and becoming complacent. Thanks for the help, mate. Cheers, and keep up the great content.

D."

"DSO,

My wife and I have been in marriage counseling for over a year. It was my idea. I was tired of zero love and affection from her. Zero sex. The good part about going to counseling is that we really open up and talk about everything. We both feel better and closer after the sessions. We hold each other more. Every time we go to the counselor, she asks about how things are in the bedroom. My wife refuses to say anything about it other than she is not ready… and I end up just taking over the session and telling her how much it hurts me. The counselor actually agreed with me that withholding intimacy is a passive-aggressive way of her resenting me. She admits that she resents me but she doesn't ever agree to have sex. So we're at a standstill.

I saw your book on Facebook and bought it. Everything made sense. It finally all clicked. I went to the counselor with her again and said that I was tired of talking about things and that I was going to work on me instead of US from now on. The counselor liked my thoughts and my 'new energy,' but my wife didn't. She was just more resentful, and it seemed to set us back even more.

I told myself that I was giving your ideas three months before I went to an attorney to talk about divorce. By month number two my wife came into the shower with me one morning and gave me oral sex. She hasn't done that since we started dating. I couldn't believe it. That same night she put the kids to bed and then told me to go to the bedroom for a surprise. I was amazed. My first thought was that I really needed to buy DSO a beer!

I asked my wife why her sudden change of heart. She said she finally felt like I wasn't just all about sex but instead about our marriage and becoming a better couple. I was shocked. I was actually more selfish than I've ever been and she saw it as me working on us. Wow. I will never understand women.

Thank you for all you do. You saved our marriage. Let's get together for that beer!
J."

"DSO,

To make a very long story short, I was the perfect Nice Guy to my wife for ten years. In the last five years or so, I'd say we have had sex probably ten times total. She has been obviously turned off completely by me but swears it's not my fault she doesn't want to have sex.

I read your book, stopped making the Mistakes, and this past month we've had more sex than the past five years total. Swear to God.

I was pretty angry at first. I've been told by her that I need to be nice and live by 'happy wife, happy life,' and she always secretly hated it. As soon as I grew a backbone, she suddenly liked me again. Not sure why she didn't just tell me what she wanted, but I also know that she's not a man so she won't do that. She'll just test me instead.

I hope everything keeps going in the same direction. After living like this I can't go back to the old me again.
Thanks for writing the book and showing up on my Facebook feed.

L."

"DSO,

My story is probably not like the rest of them. I was in a sexless marriage for years. I read your book and it really hit home for me. I did everything wrong. You also made me realize that my gut may have been right all along and my wife was cheating on me. Looks like there were at least two guys she was seeing but probably more. We divorced and she robbed me blind. I do get to see the kids half the time so not all is lost.

There is good news though. I started dating and using what I learned from your book and the sex has been crazy. The girl I'm seeing now actually said to me that she's glad I'm a real man and can actually make a decision. She says all the other men she dated acted like girls. I just had to laugh. I used to be one of those guys.

Thank you for all your hard work.

F."

"DSO,

I thought you might like this story. After our last coaching session, I did what you said and decided to not be scared to talk and be a little flirty with other women in front of my wife. As you know, because of a previous huge drama moment we had early in our marriage, that was something I've always been scared of.

We had my company's Christmas party last month. There was a very attractive single manager of the company who was being especially friendly to me. She's about ten years older than me but could easily pass for younger. Drop dead gorgeous. Every guy at the office talks about her. She's divorced. My wife has said before that she doesn't like her, which is code for her being jealous.

As you know, our sex life has improved a great deal since I put into use the things I learned from you and the DB Fix. I still wanted to have that crazy sex life we had before we had kids. We came close, but my wife still seemed to be holding back and not letting her freak flag fly again.

Well, we went to the party and the attractive manager lady was there. After a few drinks that night she wouldn't leave me alone. She literally hung on to me all night. My coworkers thought it was the funniest thing they ever saw. My wife sure didn't think so! She didn't make a scene, but you could tell that she was upset all night. On the drive home, she said, 'Your friend sure seems to like you an awful lot.' I just smiled and said, 'Well, I can't blame her.' That was NOT something I would ever normally say. Old me would explain that she was ugly, she meant nothing, I only have eyes for my wife, she is crazy to even be a little jealous… I'll skip the dirty details, but we had the best sex of our entire relationship that night. I still can't believe the things my wife was willing and able to do. Unfuckingbelieveable. Thank you, DSO! I'm so glad I found your book and got the help from you I needed.

Q."

"DSO,

Thanks so much for writing The DB Fix. That book was

exactly what I needed for my marriage. My wife actually found the book on my iPad and got very upset. She cried and said she felt horrible for not wanting sex and she wishes she did. I just told her I understood her point and I was done pressuring her to do something she didn't want to do. I said I was doing the hard work for me, not for us. She was angry after that (she said it sounded like I wanted to divorce) and didn't talk to me for a week. I was actually pretty damn close to divorcing her at that point. I met with an attorney to see what it would cost me. Let's just say it wasn't good and I decided to give my marriage another chance. LOL.

It took probably three months until my wife woke up one morning crying and saying that she felt bad for how she had been treating me and she saw how hard I had been working on myself and our marriage. She tried to give me oral, and it took all of my energy to stop her. I told her I didn't want pity sex with a crying woman, I wanted a wife that really WANTS me and that I was hoping that would be her. She cried and begged me not to divorce her. She said if I didn't want sex then what else was there for her to do? I just told her that maybe she should put the same work into herself and our marriage as I had. She said I was right and that she would.

She was true to her word. She joined the same gym I go to. She stopped all junk food. She dresses sexier. She lost forty-nine pounds. She's happier around the house. She treats me with love instead of treating me like an annoying child. For the first time in our marriage, I feel like she's chasing and

trying to impress me instead of the other way around.
We started having sex again and it's been fantastic. Right
now I have zero complaints about our marriage.
Thanks again for writing the book!

E."

From our Private Forums in the HFM Brotherhood group:

"I thought I'd post an update tonight because there was
something that was said that really stood out, which I'll get
to.

Last night we were watching TV, and she was nodding
off. It got to be about 12:30 and she said she was going to
lay down. So, I said, 'Yes me too, I have an early morning.'
(Gonna hit the gym early because they're finally open.) We
lay down in bed and chit-chatted for a bit while she was
nodding in and out. She finally said, 'I'm going to fall asleep
unless you're going to keep me up.' Even though I knew
what she was getting at, I replied with, 'How am I going
to keep you up?' She said, 'Oh, I don't know...' so I just
said, 'Yea, me either. I'm going to bed too. I have an early
morning.' I could have probably initiated things because
she gave me the green light, but I knew it wasn't worth it
because she was really tired and wasn't all there.

Fast forward to today. She made several sexual comments
to me all day and told me how she wanted it the night
before but she was just too tired. Then she proceeded to
tell me she was fully rested tonight. So, obviously I just

played everything smooth all day and didn't even act at all bothered by her.

Later on in the evening, she started drinking some wine. We decided we were going to go out to a local pizza place and get some dinner. The kids didn't want to get off the Xbox, so she and I just went. Refer back to the beginning when I said she said something that stood out. Well, on the way to dinner, she said, 'You know, I really just think I needed you to be more of a lover to me to get me turned on and that's what you've been doing.' Then right after that she reached over, unzipped my pants, and started giving me road head. Holy fuck. LOL. She's never done that, not once.

Fast forward, we ate dinner and the entire time all she was talking about was fucking. All I could think about was who the hell switched my wife out LOL. Well, we got home, and she took the kids' food upstairs, then she came downstairs, ripped my pants off, and started going to town again. Next thing you know we're upstairs in our bedroom and the rest is history. She's now sleeping like a baby lol.

At this point, I'm not even sure what I've done but I've just done basically what the book says to do in my own way and it's worked a damn miracle. That's two crazy weekends in a row.

Sorry for the long post, just wanted to give an update and hopefully, some encouragement for everyone to keep it up because this shit works.

M."

"I'm really grateful & thankful for DSO's book randomly popping up on my FB feed one day. Without it, I really don't think I'd still be married for eighteen years. I love my wife, but I was so frustrated with my marriage and lack of intimacy. Feeling rejected and unloved and, most of all, unable to figure out why that was. That was the key. His book gave me simple, understandable reasons and unapologetic answers to why things weren't going well in my marriage. I'm a regular nice guy, so I need simple straight talk and I can't tell you how much better this easily readable book was so much more effective than the hundreds of hours spent in individual and couples counseling I did for years—and not to mention thousands of dollars cheaper. This book has made me a better man and has made my marriage much more fun, enjoyable, and sexually satisfying...FOR BOTH OF US! She's more loving, playful, appreciative, supportive, and affectionate. Her mood is elevated, her attitude towards me is positive and affirming, and it's because I'm a better man. My only regret is that I didn't read it ten years ago when things in my marriage started to change. I will always feel indebted to him for making a lasting impression on me so that I could make the life I wanted with my wife and kids.

J."

"I was lost and thought I had tried everything. I think I Googled something like 'dead bedroom' and it led me to the book. I read the reviews and couldn't wait to get my hands on it for myself. I implemented the rules, and I can honestly say that I instantly started seeing success. It has been a few months post-DBF and I can genuinely say that we are the happiest we have ever been. I am stronger, more confident, and overall content. The private group and the Brotherhood are priceless and an endless source of support and information.

N."

"I have a love/hate relationship with The Dead Bedroom Fix. I love it because it has changed the way I look at my relationship. I hate it because it was a kick in the nuts and made me admit my failures.

My behavior has changed towards her, and hers towards me. I've implemented the changes, and see that although my bedroom seems dead, it's more on life support with signs of coming out of it because of what I have learned.

I pass most of her shit tests, call her on her rejection BS with humor, notice more that needs to be done around the house, and do it before she mentions it and without wanting accolades.

We're butting heads with leadership, with her acquiescing more (albeit small things) to me.

She's walking around naked more around me now that I've taken her off the pedestal and I'm treating her like a person. I know it's going to be a long road, but thanks to The Dead Bedroom Fix, it'll be a smooth road.

J."

"Just wanted to show my appreciation to the DSO for introducing me to the Dead Bedroom Fix and getting me into a community of recovering Nice Guys. Not to mention it was my gateway to other books like No More Mr. Nice Guy. The way it's changed my life over the past three months is really incredible. It hasn't just changed my sexual life with my wife, but it's also affected my daily happiness and assertiveness at work.

I'm thankful for all of the harsh truths and reality checks. Somehow, just being subscribed to the HFM Brotherhood (have been for a month now) doesn't seem like contribution enough. Let me know if there's ever anything I can help out with.

A."

"DSO's no-nonsense, straight-talk writing style is the swift kick in the ASS that men need!

Men have been lied to and not taught how to really keep intimacy alive. Society tells you to give her everything she wants, submit to her demands, solve all her problems, and exhibit inherently feminine behavior.

DSO debunks several generations of progressive myths and lies and realigns the reader with the animalistic, primal impulses and how they apply to a marriage or long-term relationship in the twenty-first century.

My bedroom was not dead but it was not trending in the

right direction. I was being passive, agreeable, and needy. My demanding work and the stressors of life had beaten us both down. I was letting her lead.

I read the book, and within two weeks I had excellent results. Fast forward two months later and I have not had this much sex since I was in my early twenties. This is the most impactful book I've read in the last decade. This is a must-buy for all men who look to drastically improve not only their bedroom but their marriage.

Thank you, DSO!

J."

"I don't recall how I stumbled across the HFM Brotherhood. I joined the group and read everyone's posts and comments for a month. The wife and I have been fighting the worst we ever have. I was insulting her and screaming at her all the time. She was ready to leave me, and I was ready to leave her.

I ordered the book and read it in one night— and what an eye-opener. This book made me realize what a bad husband and lover I had become, and no wonder my wife didn't want to make love to me. I realized I needed to fix myself, so I started walking six kilometers every morning to clear my mind when I woke up. I upped it to ten kilometers in the morning to push myself more and added another three to five in the afternoons. (It's thirty to thirty-five degrees Celsius during my walks, so they are not a walk in the park, so to speak.) I then work out for thirty to forty-five minutes. Then in the afternoon, I start a project around the house and finish it: yard work, building a basketball court with the kids, painting the house. I took an online anger management course, I read self-help and improvement books in the evenings. I talk to a counselor once a week and bitch to them, not my wife.

I'm forty-three and never walked, worked out, or took care of myself. I'm now changing my diet to get that six-pack I always wanted. I'm tanning an hour a day plus the walking is helping my tan. It's only been two weeks but I'm such a different person, I talk calmly to my kids and wife, and when we don't agree I just say my point and that's it— no arguing, no more discussion. My kids take turns joining me on my daily walk;. they are enjoying their newfound Dad. My confidence is getting way better. My wife respects me more and initiated a love-making session after a massage, and she has never done that! It's only been two weeks of hard work, but I'm seeing progress. Yes, it's going to take months to get my six-pack and full confidence. Hopefully by then, my wife is jumping me and the passion has been reignited. If not, at least I gave her the best possible me and I'll be fine going forward.

Thanks, DSO for opening my eyes and helping me with that first giant step.

M."

Let me know what you think.

Shoot me an email at ralph.b@helpformen.com. I would love to hear what you thought about this book, good and bad.

THANK YOU for reading. I hope it gave you a sense of hope and strength and put you on the right path to being a better dude… and getting more ass than a toilet seat. Rock on, brother.

Ralph (a.k.a. "DSO")

Join The HFM Brotherhood!

We have a team of coaches and hundreds of men around the world JUST LIKE YOU that are standing by and waiting to help you. We get together all day every day to talk in our private forums, we chat regularly in live Zoom meetings, we get together in person… it's an amazing group of guys that I am VERY proud to be a part of. Learn more about all the benefits of joining at:

helpformen.com/join